Praise for *Partners in Literacy: A Writing Center Model for Civic Engagement*

"In the vein of scholarship like Eli Goldblatt's *Because We Live Here*, Tiffany Rousculp's *Rhetoric of Respect*, and the *Everyday Writing Center*, Brizee and Wells' *Partners in Literacy: A Writing Center Model for Civic Engagement* offers a critical intervention for bridging the comfortable confines of conventional tutoring of academic writing to liminal spaces out in a larger community where a different sort of service, learning, and educational transformation can happen and be sustained. For writing centers, labs, and studios, where community engagement (and relevance) is central to their missions, *Partners in Literacy* provides a cogent road map rooted in organic collaboration, awareness of the politics of community, and attention to the cross-currents of local institutionality and history. Brizee and Wells make tangible the legwork and lived lessons that writing center professionals would wisely heed if they seek to make effective, lasting partnerships. The text is a must-read for those in search of a model to guide their own outreach beyond campus—perhaps even within it too." —**Harry Denny**, associate professor of English and director of the Purdue Writing Lab and the Purdue OWL, Purdue University

"Partnerships between university writing programs/writing centers and the communities that they border are often fraught with logistical, ethical, and philosophical challenges. In *Partners in Literacy*, Brizee and Wells guide readers through the challenges they faced to create the Community Writing and Education Station (CWEST), which focused on online resources for both adult literacy (particularly GED exam preparation) and job placement organizations. Their account of this project, launched while both were graduate students at Purdue, offers readers every step in the processes of creating, testing, and implementing CWEST, as well as powerful reflections on the challenges of responding to the true needs of community partners. Writing programs and writing center readers, whether currently engaged in such efforts or contemplating future ones, will be very well served by this book, including the cautions and the accomplishments the authors powerfully describe." —**Neal Lerner**, Writing Program director, Northeastern University

"Wells and Brizee give readers an honest and careful account of how and what they learned from their participation as graduate students in a research partnership between the Purdue Writing Lab, the Lafayette Adult Resource Academy, and WorkOne Lafayette. They detail the ways they used that new knowledge to inform their work with community partnerships in their faculty positions post-graduation, giving credence to the claim that writing programs and writing program administrators learn from engagement." —**Shirley Rose**, professor of English and director of Writing Program, Arizona State University

Partners in Literacy

Partners in Literacy

A Writing Center Model for Civic Engagement

Allen Brizee and Jaclyn M. Wells

ROWMAN & LITTLEFIELD
Lanham • Boulder • New York • London

Published by Rowman & Littlefield
A wholly owned subsidiary of The Rowman & Littlefield Publishing Group, Inc.
4501 Forbes Boulevard, Suite 200, Lanham, Maryland 20706
www.rowman.com

Unit A, Whitacre Mews, 26-34 Stannary Street, London SE11 4AB, United Kingdom

Copyright © 2016 by Allen Brizee and Jaclyn M. Wells

All rights reserved. No part of this book may be reproduced in any form or by any electronic or mechanical means, including information storage and retrieval systems, without written permission from the publisher, except by a reviewer who may quote passages in a review.

Portions of chapters 2, 4, and 5 were revised from an earlier version originally published in *Computers and Composition: An International Journal* 32 (2014): 22-40.
Used with permission.

British Library Cataloguing in Publication Information Available

Library of Congress Cataloging-in-Publication Data Available
ISBN: 978-1-4758-2761-3 (cloth : alk. paper)
ISBN: 978-1-4758-2762-0 (pbk. : alk. paper)
ISBN: 978-1-4758-2763-7 (electronic)

∞™ The paper used in this publication meets the minimum requirements of American National Standard for Information Sciences—Permanence of Paper for Printed Library Materials, ANSI/NISO Z39.48-1992.

Printed in the United States of America

Contents

Foreword by *Tom Deans*	ix
Preface: Bridging University and Community Spaces	xi
Acknowledgments	xvii
Introduction	xix

1 Background and Methodology — 1
- The Distance Between Universities and Communities — 1
- An Engaged Course Project — 3
- The Researchers' Backgrounds — 6
- Finding a Community Partner — 13
- The Researcher's Roles in the Project — 18
- Emergent Methodology — 19

2 Community Partners and Overview of Research Methods — 21
- Reaching Out to the Community — 22
- Learning More about the Community Partners — 26
- Writing the Engagement Project — 34
- Research Methods and Seeking IRB Approval — 36
- Funding the Project — 39

3 Methods and Findings from Stage One: Developing the GED Resources — 43
- A Picture of a Community Education Program: Initial Research Findings — 44
- Drafting the GED Materials — 48
- First Reactions to the GED Resources: A Focus Group — 49

	After the Focus Group: Initial Revisions to the GED Resources	51
	Instructor Response to the GED Resources: Round Two Interviews and Observations	54
4	**Methods and Findings from Stages Two and Three: Developing the ESL and Job Document Resources**	**63**
	Revising the Resources and Posting Them to the Purdue OWL	64
	Generation One Testing	67
	Working with WorkOne	73
	Generation Two Testing	79
5	**Discussion and Key Takeaways**	**85**
	Jaclyn's Reflections	86
	Allen's Reflections	94
	Key Takeaways	103
6	**Engagement as Professional Work**	**105**
	Engaged Scholarship: How the CWEST Informs Allen's Community-Based Work in Baltimore	106
	Diverse Roles and Responsibilities: How the CWEST Informs Jaclyn's Writing Center Work	115

Epilogue: Looking Back, Looking Forward	127
Appendix: Chapter Heuristic Questions	135
Research Protocols	140
Observational Protocol for First LARA Observations	141
Observational Protocol for Second LARA Observations	142
CWEST LARA Usability Test Protocol	143
LARA Instructor Interview Script	146
WorkOne Express Interview Questions	147
WorkOne Express Usability Testing	147
References	151
Index	155
About the Authors	165

Foreword
Tom Deans

When I first ventured into university/community partnerships twenty years ago, I didn't give a thought to the potential of writing centers for such work. Instead my attention was trained on writing courses; and for me, courses remain vital—indeed, even the community literacy project that inspired this book had its origins in a course on public rhetoric. But after having spent the last ten years as the director of a university writing center, I'm convinced, as are Allen Brizee and Jaclyn M. Wells, that writing centers might be even more promising sites for civic engagement.

It's one thing to say that. It's another to live it. It is still another to show us how you did it. This book—grounded in both story and theory—does all three.

When I think of writing centers, I see one-on-one peer tutoring—two students around a table, leaning into a text, in animated conversation. And that is (mostly) how it plays out every day on my rural, residential campus. So eight years ago, when considering how our center should engage in outreach, my natural impulse was to double down on that signature practice. We opted to work with local middle and high schools, assisting them in launching their own peer writing centers, and this has proven to be good and worthwhile work. We're proud of the vibrant regional network of writing centers that has emerged. Yet, reading this book made me realize that reproducing the university model is but one way to go, and one that betrays a certain lack of imagination.

By turning their attention to adult education, local literacy initiatives, digital technologies, and online pedagogies, Brizee and Wells enact a venturesome ethical imagination. They document the lifecycle of an authentic project, one born of their personal commitments, shaped by local circumstances, and informed by scholarship. That account is instructive in its own right. Yet, what makes this book especially relevant to those contemplating a move from the writing center to the public sphere is how Brizee and Wells share their experiences with—and strategies for—relationship building, design thinking, and empirical methods.

No community project will unfold quite like any other—and as their story shows, no project will go quite as planned. Yet, relationship building, design thinking, and empirical methods can and should inform every such initiative. They are the gifts of this book.

Thomas Deans
University of Connecticut

Preface
Bridging University and Community Spaces

A collaborative spirit guides this book and the civic engagement project it describes. *Partners in Literacy* marks a collaboration between two thinkers whose mutual interests in writing centers and university-community engagement resulted in a longstanding, productive partnership. The three-year engagement project described here, the Community Writing and Education Station (CWEST), fostered collaboration between university and community educators and worked toward improving local adult literacy education.

The CWEST project joined Purdue University's Writing Lab with two community-based groups in Lafayette, Indiana: the Lafayette Adult Resource Academy (LARA), an adult literacy program, and the local branch of WorkOne, the Indiana employment agency. The variety of skills, experiences, and expertise represented by the three contributors—the Writing Lab, LARA, and WorkOne—produced tangible and substantial improvements to local literacy education and expanded the scope of the university writing center.

In short, what the collaborators did together, they could never have accomplished alone. The project's main deliverable was a new space on the Purdue Online Writing Lab (OWL) dedicated to engagement, but outcomes far exceed this one product. The relationships fostered were just as significant, if not more so, than the products created. In presenting the story of the CWEST, *Partners in Literacy* makes one overarching argument and focuses on two ideas.

The primary argument is that writing centers can be effective spaces from which to work with local communities and that this work need not be limited to opening one-on-one tutoring sessions for the community. To support this argument, the authors focus on two ideas: (1) the iterative process and the empirical methods that guided the CWEST project and (2) the personal instigation and personal relationships that were the glue that held the project together. Also interwoven throughout the book are the theories and relevant scholarship that provide the full story of the CWEST.

Collaboration among educators from different contexts greatly influenced the CWEST project. After meeting with the community partners, the researchers noticed a major gap in the Purdue Writing Lab's resources. Specifically, the Purdue OWL offered literacy resources for students and teachers of diverse levels and educational contexts, but left out one major group: teachers and students of adult literacy. The OWL contained numerous resources for college students writing academic papers, for example, but no resources for students preparing to take the GED, the high-school diploma equivalency test.

From community educators, the researchers also learned that the Purdue OWL was not the only online space of its kind that overlooked the needs of this group of students and teachers. Very few free online resources existed for adult literacy students and teachers. Bolstered with general knowledge of these gaps in resources, enthusiastic university and community participants, and a sincere desire to collaborate, the researchers' goals for the project became clearer: Work together to address significant gaps and improve university-community relations at the same time.

Of course, this type of work is rarely so simple, particularly not the difficult, complex work of literacy education and university-community collaboration. The researchers might have attempted to deny or eliminate the obstacles and complexities central to civic engagement. Instead, the project quickly focused on addressing roadblocks collaboratively with community members, particularly fellow educators. This model was influenced by Flower's (2008) claim that "rhetorically based collaborative community literacy *starts* in inquiry" (p. 230).

With inquiry at the center, the project's goals became more complicated than "create new resources" or "broaden the writing center's scope" or even "improve university-community relations" (goals that are themselves plenty complicated). The larger purpose became developing and addressing areas of inquiry *with* the community partners as Deans (2010) advocated (pp. 108–10), an approach Ernest L. Boyer (1990) called the "scholarship of engagement."

The CWEST project began, then, in inquiry. At the project's earliest stages, writing center administrators and educators met with the community organizations to determine needs, raise questions, and brainstorm ideas about local literacy issues. As collaborators made decisions about the project, they continued to raise questions, find answers, and revise goals. This work was recursive and often messy.

In writing this book, the authors seek to bring that full process—messiness and all—to light. Too often, the reporting of community-based work skips the details of engagement, speaking only to the big picture of collaboration and to the work's major phases or research findings. By leaving out parts of the process, including the meetings and documents that make collaboration happen, organizers of community-based work can unwittingly tell stories of engagement that are far more simple and linear than they were in reality.

These simplified tales not only fail to acknowledge the complexity of civic engagement, but also leave readers ignorant of the details about how to engage their communities. These omissions can leave readers unprepared to handle the inevitable challenges and even total failures that can occur during community-based work. Recently, scholars have called for inquiry into the shortcomings and failures of civic engagement (Cushman and Grabill, 2009; Rumsey and Nihiser, 2011). The authors hope to respond to these calls by telling the complete story of the CWEST.

In the CWEST project, collaborative processes of inquiry and planning occurred through meetings and proposals and through qualitative and quantitative research. Empirical methods, many borrowed from technical communication, were used at all stages of the CWEST project to investigate the process *and* products of engagement. Throughout the book, the authors argue that formal research should address persistent problems with community engagement, including unsustainability and lack of clear benefits for the community partner.

By formally investigating community-based work and using findings to improve that work, community researchers and organizers can develop more effective projects that address community needs and that outlast initial enthusiasm. In some ways, the book's discussion of research resembles its discussion of engagement: The focus is on *process*, including the process of using findings to improve the CWEST project, in the hopes that readers will better understand how research-driven writing center engagement can look in practice.

At the same time, understanding the CWEST project means more than understanding the research methods and findings, the "head" part of the work. It means also understanding the people and feelings, the "heart" of the work. The book attempts to provide a full picture of both the head and heart of the CWEST project. As mentioned previously, the personal relationships created during the CWEST project were often even more powerful than the products created. These relationships are one example of the project's "heart."

Due to the complex and longitudinal nature of the project, the typical "research book" organization does not offer the best option for telling the full story. Instead, this book tells the CWEST's story in an accessible and personal manner so that readers may gain insight into details often omitted in research books following an IMRaD approach (introduction, methods, research findings, and discussion). Nonetheless, readers are still able to "raid" the book to obtain specific information, such as theories, research methods, findings, and conclusions of the study, by using the table of contents, headings, and subheadings.

Instead of the typical research book, the authors use a blended approach, or a research narrative, to provide the full story of the CWEST. This blended genre mixes personal reflection with more cut and dry research prose. Inspired by works such as Shirley Brice Heath's (1993) *Ways with Words: Language, Life, and Works in Communities and Classrooms*, Paula Mathieu's (2005) *Tactics of Hope*, and Harry C. Denny's (2010) *Facing the Center: Toward an Identity Politics of One-to-One Mentoring*, the book blends narrative with research in a practical yet readable genre.

In some sections of the book, the authors speak with a unified voice to reflect their combined experiences, but in other sections, the authors speak with individual voices to communicate their different perspectives. The goal is to interweave two experiences with one project and explain how that project has impacted the authors' current work as faculty members. Additionally, the authors hope their individual perspectives help show how scholarly engagement can inform different areas of faculty work, including teaching, administration, and service.

Included in the book are ample visuals to explain the project's models, deliverables, and findings and to help readers understand the CWEST and its outcomes. To date, no other book-length works present this type of information in this manner. So while the number of books on writing centers increases, along with the number of books on community work, *Partners in Literacy* considers writing centers in a different and more civic way and blends the two scholarly areas together.

Partners in Literacy is written for many audiences. Specifically, the authors hope that writing center administrators and tutors will find the information applicable and compelling, especially if they are interested in public rhetoric and civic engagement. To be clear, however, this book does not discuss writing center theory and practice in a way that focuses on peer-to-peer pedagogy. Rather, the book discusses how writing centers can make the public turn and integrate civic engagement into their efforts.

Nonetheless, a central theme of the book is that the "power with" (*logos dunamis*) versus "power over" (*logos hegemon*) approach of writing centers provides guidance for reciprocal university-community partnerships that can foster positive outcomes. In considering the wide variety of situations facing writing centers at different institutions, the authors have also tried to present information in a flexible and scalable manner. The book offers information about how readers might tailor community work to their specific contexts in the epilogue. A list of generative questions, organized to supplement the book chapters, is included in the appendix.

Though the book is written with a writing center audience in mind, other readers will find value in its discussion of engagement and research. As noted above, the book includes information about important, but often omitted, aspects of civic engagement, such as the process for obtaining funding, the Institutional Review Board (IRB) approval process, and project management. The authors hope that many readers will benefit from learning about this full, messy process.

More specifically, faculty members in rhetoric and composition and graduate students interested in public rhetoric and service-learning will find much to explore here regarding university-community boundaries and how writing studies might overcome these obstacles. The full story of engagement and research may also be useful to graduate students who are interested in taking on similar projects in the present and in the future but may feel unsure of the particulars of such work.

Acknowledgments

This book is dedicated to our late parents, Bonnie Wells, Paula Brizee, and Harry Brizee.

We are indebted to many mentors, colleagues, and friends for their feedback and encouragement. Thank you to reviewers who have read portions of the book and provided insightful suggestions. Thanks especially to Michael Spooner and Victor Villanueva for helping to shape our ideas and the direction of the book.

We would also like to acknowledge our incredible mentors at Purdue for supporting and guiding this project from its beginnings. Thank you especially to our mentor and dear friend, the late Linda Bergmann. Without Linda's generosity, patience, and wisdom, this project would have never gotten off the ground, much less resulted in a published book. We are sad that Linda is not able to see the book in print, but we are grateful always to have worked with her and aware of the many ways she continues to shape our thinking and our work. We would also like to thank Purdue mentors Patricia Sullivan, Irwin "Bud" Weiser, Shirley Rose, Richard Johnson-Sheehan, and Tony Silva for their help and encouragement.

Our friends from Purdue also provided much needed support and feedback as we worked through our ideas. Special thanks to the members of our cohort, Danielle Cordaro, Dana Driscoll, Karen Schiler, Morgan Sousa, and the late Jo Doran. The many conversations shared with this special group have shaped our ideas immeasurably, and clearly, the laughs along the way have motivated us to keep working. Finally, we would like to thank the teachers and staff at the Lafayette Adult Resource Academy and WorkOne for a truly inspiring collaboration and for all of the work they do to support adult literacy in Lafayette.

Jaclyn would also like to thank colleagues from the University of Southern Indiana and the University of Alabama at Birmingham for their help and encouragement. Thanks especially to UAB Professional Writing colleagues Cynthia Ryan, Bruce McComiskey, Chris Minnix, and Jeff Bacha for talking out ideas along the way and to the writing center family for providing constant inspiration. For their encouragement and support, she is also indebted to Jim Wells, Mitch Wells, and Kathy and Rick Bacha. Jaclyn also thanks her fur-buddy Travis for always keeping her feet warm while she writes. Finally, Jaclyn would like to thank Jeff Bacha for all of his love, good humor, and support, including never saying "no" to the question, "hey, can you read this paragraph really quick?"

Allen would like to thank Jim Dubinsky, Eva Brumberger, and Paul Heilker for their support early in his career at Virginia Tech. He would also like to thank colleagues at Loyola University, Maryland for their generous help: Cindy Moore, Peggy O'Neill, Megan Linz Dickinson, Erin O'Keefe, Kate Figiel-Miller, and Robin Crews. Allen would also like to thank his service-learning students, the Richnor Springs Neighborhood Association, and staff and clients at GEDCO/CARES Career Connections for their wonderful collaboration. He would also like to thank Becky Wright Brizee, Abby and Steve Rawlins, for their love and guidance. Allen must also thank all of the special canine family members who have always had time for a warm snuggle during bouts of writer's block: Barkley, Dory, Beatrice, Daisy, Ginny, and Doogle.

Introduction
Chapter Overviews

To provide some insight into the authors' "personal instigation," as Sullivan and Porter (1997) described in *Opening Spaces: Writing Technologies and Critical Research Practices*, chapter 1 overviews their initial interest in the project, as well as the parts of their journeys through education that influenced this work. The authors speak with separate voices here to more clearly describe their backgrounds as activist-scholars, and they return to a unified voice to explain the beginnings of collaboration with LARA and WorkOne.

The final section of chapter 1 outlines the nascent methodology that emerged from the CWEST project and that in retrospect has proven valuable in guiding the authors' current efforts in civic engagement. Throughout the remainder of the book, the authors return to and expand on this methodology to help situate readers in the project's process and align the work with the different steps of the methodology.

Chapter 2 details the early steps in collaborating with LARA/WorkOne and provides information about these community partners. Chapter 2 also explains how the researchers and community partners worked together to write the project into existence. This part of the chapter discusses often-neglected subjects like project proposals, IRBs, and funding. Finally, this part of the chapter offers an overview and rationale for the project's research methods.

Chapter 3 explains the iterative and participatory process used to develop the online GED, ESL, and job search resources, housed at the time in the Engagement section of the Purdue OWL, that were the main products of the CWEST. This discussion focuses on the early stages of work on the GED resources. These early stages involved interviews and focus groups. Chapter 3 also presents findings from this first stage of collaboration.

Chapter 4 continues this discussion by providing information on the CWEST ESL resources. Included here is explanation of the usability testing that the researchers conducted on both the GED and ESL resources after they were posted to the OWL. The chapter also discusses the process of revising the CWEST and developing the job search materials. Finally, chapter 4 presents findings from these second and third stages of work.

In chapter 5, the authors speak with separate voices to reflect on their individual experiences with the CWEST, including the project's successes and limitations. They explain their impressions of the impact the CWEST had on LARA and WorkOne. The authors also reflect on how the CWEST influenced their own experiences toward the end of graduate work. These reflections may interest graduate students who are thinking about doing community-based work, perhaps as part of their coursework or thesis or dissertation research.

The authors also speak with separate voices in chapter 6, where they discuss the influence of the CWEST on their current work as faculty members. Included are specific connections from the CWEST to the authors' recent projects and explanation of how they have attempted to build on the CWEST's small successes, incorporate what they learned into their current faculty responsibilities, and address the project's shortcomings and limitations. These reflections may interest faculty members who are thinking about doing community-based work but are unsure of how to manage it alongside teaching, research, service, and administration.

The epilogue draws together the authors' past and current experiences and looks ahead to needs and possibilities in community-based research. Within this conclusion is consideration of how writing centers can not only do more than just house community-based projects, but also provide philosophies of engagement and action-focused research that translate effectively to community-based work. Conversely, the authors argue, writing centers can borrow and benefit from many of the philosophies behind community engagement and research.

Lastly, the book concludes with some reflection on how writing centers and community engagement projects face many of the same challenges as programs and resources that, unfortunately, are often regarded as "extra" instead of central to educational institutions. *Partners in Literacy* does not offer simple answers to these challenges. Instead, the authors hope that readers can learn from the candid account of one project's successes and failures and apply these lessons to their own work in their own ways.

Chapter 1

Background and Methodology

This book leads readers through the entire process of a three-year engagement project—from the very beginning, through the findings, successes, and failures, to the outcomes and impacts on the authors' work today. Throughout this account are the messy and complicated parts of the process that the literature of community engagement often omits. These messy, complicated parts of the process are important to examine so that the field of writing studies might help foster valuable, sustainable, and honest collaboration between universities and communities.

Writing centers, because of their ability to form stable spaces in the midst of messy, complicated situations, can help develop and maintain sustained relationships between college and community. With the goal of sharing the full process of this project, therefore, chapter 1 begins at the first stages of the CWEST project: the authors' personal instigation and collaboration. Included within this discussion are some of the theories that influenced the collaboration and the project.

THE DISTANCE BETWEEN UNIVERSITIES AND COMMUNITIES

The CWEST was motivated partly by the desire to address common university-community boundaries that impede collaboration. Two years of attending Purdue University (and other institutions before it) provided Allen and Jaclyn with plenty of opportunities to observe the distance between a university and a community. These collective observations formed part of the CWEST project's personal instigation, to borrow from Sullivan and Porter (1997).

Even writing centers, with their missions of outreach and collaboration, very often seem distanced from their surrounding communities. Outreach projects spring up in writing centers, including those in which Jaclyn and Allen had worked, but engaging the community seems often more like an occasional "special project" instead of a sustained commitment. Both the university, including writing centers, and the community could benefit from and contribute to greater—and sustained—engagement.

Many circumstances suggest a distance between Purdue and the community to its east, Lafayette, Indiana. The two are physically separated by the Wabash River, which runs between West Lafayette and Lafayette. Just as visitors to West Lafayette must cross the Wabash to experience what lies beyond Purdue, casual observers may notice similar boundaries by driving through typical college towns and crossing whatever streets, rivers, or monuments mark crossing to "the other side" beyond the university.

Scholars like Ellen Cushman (1996) and David Coogan (2005) have noted such physical signs of university-community boundaries. Philosophical lines may be less obvious, but boundaries and tensions between the town and gown commonly parallel the physical distance between them and define university-community relationships. These physical and philosophical distances both create and are exacerbated by the lack of sustained community engagement.

In a graduate-level public rhetoric course—the course in which the CWEST project originally formed—one major indicator of the educational distance between Purdue and the Lafayette community came to light. The professor, Patricia Sullivan, distributed a recently published newspaper article that compared the performance of public schools on the "Purdue Side" to public schools "Over the River" in 2009. This article formed a major part of the authors' personal instigation to foster collaboration between Purdue and Lafayette.

The comparison between schools was a staggering 95.4 percent graduation rate at the high school on the "Purdue side" versus 65 percent at the largest high school "over the river" on the Lafayette side (Indiana Department of Education, 2009). Learning these startling statistics greatly increased the authors' interest in developing partnerships between the university and the community. More specifically, these statistics suggested the need for community-university collaboration that would improve local education for those not directly affiliated with Purdue.

Further, the specific nature of the statistics shaped what would become the CWEST project. The statistics raised some questions: What was happening to the 35 percent of students not graduating from Lafayette's largest high school? Where were they going? Further, could university-community collaboration help support these students, perhaps by contributing to the type of second chance that Mike Rose (2012) describes in *Back to School*?

Lack of engagement between educators creates many of the problems, including the great disparity between schools like those in West Lafayette and Lafayette. Further, university-community boundaries parallel and intensify the distance between educators of different levels and contexts. Unfortunately, few efforts join educators in productive, mutually beneficial collaborations that might close the gap between them.

Further, elimination of direct federal funding for the National Writing Project (NWP) in 2011 reminded us that existing efforts are vulnerable. Many NWP sites closed or drastically scaled back, including well-established sites at universities that had long supported collaboration among educators in their regions and communities. Importantly, lack of university-community collaboration does not necessarily stem from a lack of willingness to work together; outcry about NWP funding makes this clear.

For the university members, challenges to civic engagement relate to the funding, scholarship, and journal hierarchies, as described in the 2007 University of Utah "University Neighborhood Partners" program report; these hierarchies discourage community-based work. Simply put, many corners of academe just don't value community work in the same way they do other types of scholarship. For the community members, limited funding, resources, and time hamstring efforts to work with local universities.

Despite the challenges, university-community collaboration does happen. Many scholars in rhetoric, composition, professional writing, and writing centers have worked to address university-community boundaries, foster mutually beneficial relationships between the university and community, and improve local education through collaboration between university and community members.

In addition to Cushman and Coogan, scholars like Linda Flower, Eli Goldblatt, Paul Heilker, Thomas Deans, J. Blake Scott and Melody Bowden, Jeffrey Grabill, and Michele Simmons teach, research, and write toward decreasing the pervasive gaps between universities and communities. Further, writing center scholars like James Jesson, Frankie Condon, and Linda Bergmann have addressed how writing centers can improve their work and support the community by expanding their reach beyond the university.

Learning about these scholars and their work motivated Allen and Jaclyn to think about developing similar work at Purdue and in Lafayette. The next section describes these early motivations and work in more detail.

AN ENGAGED COURSE PROJECT

The CWEST project began in a fall 2008 graduate seminar on public rhetoric. Jaclyn and Allen were both in the third year of Purdue's PhD program in rhetoric and composition, and for both, the seminar was one of the last courses they would take before starting the dissertation stage. Studying together in a close cohort for more than two years—an experience that included surviving coursework and preliminary exams—partly enabled the collaboration. In short, the authors knew each other well and were able to use this knowledge to begin collaborating on what would become the CWEST project.

More specifically, the authors were aware not only of their common academic interests in writing centers, service-learning, and technology, but also of each other's backgrounds and how they influenced their perspectives on teaching, learning, and serving. Jaclyn knew that Allen had taken a rather circuitous route through the education system, and Allen knew that Jaclyn was stubbornly proud of her working-class roots. These backgrounds and perspectives influenced the project's personal instigation and shaped its goals from the very beginning.

Allen and Jaclyn learned early in the semester that the public rhetoric course would require an extended public engagement project that could be completed collaboratively. When they learned this, they thought immediately of their mutual and complementary interests. As this conversation progressed, they learned that their goals for the project were compatible, just like their interests.

Many students in the course were planning fascinating projects that studied various public rhetorics and public rhetorical movements. Inspired by work like Jenny Edbauer's (2005) research on the "Keep Austin Weird" campaign, other students would take the course's complex theories on rhetoric and the public and apply them to little studied texts and movements. Though Jaclyn and Allen both found these projects important, they shared a desire to engage with the public more than such work might allow. For the project, both wanted to *do* something *with* the community.

Despite enthusiasm for working with the public, the potential perils and pitfalls of community engagement are clear to most people who, like the authors, have been a teacher, student, or community member or "townie" (sometimes all at once). Growing up in a college town, Jaclyn was familiar from an early age with the university's scattered attempts at engagement. Similarly, Allen's background with adult education in his high-school years left him with an enduring awareness of class and race issues that could brutally divide young people's learning experiences.

Living in Lafayette, both Allen and Jaclyn perceived tensions between the community and university and heard stories about shoddy service projects that only compounded those bad feelings. While teaching at Purdue, both authors had been involved with service-learning projects that, while generally successful, were of the short, "hit-it-and-quit it" variety that Cushman (2002) describes in "Sustainable Service-Learning Programs."

In addition to Cushman, scholars like Coogan, among many others, have warned of the problems that often plague even the most well-intentioned community-based work. Problems include lack of sustainability, insensitivity to the community's actual needs, and incomplete work. The university-community tensions that engagement attempts to address can actually be compounded by irresponsible, unsustainable, or poorly executed projects, as Flower (2008) describes in *Community Literacy and the Rhetoric of Public Engagement*.

Among such tensions include the feeling that the university is attempting to rescue or educate the community, the charity approach that Jim Dubinsky (2002) admonishes so thoughtfully in "Service-Learning as a Path to Virtue: The Ideal Orator in Professional Communication." Jaclyn and Allen so feared the potential for swooping in to rescue the community that early conversations about the CWEST created a new word that would carry throughout the project: "swoopy," or "swoopiness." As in, "Do you think this aspect of the project could be swoopy?" Or "We don't want to swoop here."

To avoid "swooping," the CWEST would need to be collaborative and research based. Informed by scholarship like Robert Johnson's (1998) *The User-Centered Approach*, and Simmons and Grabill's (2007) "Toward a Civic Rhetoric for Technologically and Scientifically Complex Places," a mixed-methods methodological framework formed a core part of the project: the participatory and empirical approach that worked toward effective collaboration between the community and university partners.

This approach, which could also be called community-based research or participatory civic engagement, as outlined by Brizee (2014) in his article on the CWEST project, helps university partners avoid imposing themselves onto community partners. The authors also hoped that this approach would give voice to those who are so often ignored in complex research projects—the community members themselves. The goal of the project was to take a systematic approach to working with community partners to build knowledge *with* them, as Deans (2010) advocated in "English Studies and Public Service" (pp. 108–10).

In the following sections, the authors reflect on their backgrounds in order to help readers better understand their personal instigation in the CWEST project. In particular, Jaclyn and Allen's nontraditional educational paths, class identities, and prior experiences with community service contributed to their desire to collaborate and build knowledge with the community. As the reflections and stories are personal, the authors use the first person to share them.

THE RESEARCHERS' BACKGROUNDS

Jaclyn

My first experiences with community service were in high school. In addition to serving sporadically for various community organizations, I volunteered during my freshman and sophomore years at the local nursing home where both my mother and grandmother would later stay. Every Sunday morning for two years, my dad would drop me off and then retrieve me a couple of hours later. On the drive home, I would regale him with stories of calling bingo numbers, talking to my favorite resident, Doris, and carefully negotiating narrow hallways as I wheeled around the residents.

I would love to write that my time in the nursing home was motivated by my desire to help others and marked the beginning of a life dedicated to service. Most readers—and probably *any* reader who has known a fourteen-year-old—would very quickly smell the bull. Truthfully, my service at that age was motivated primarily by one desire: to build my résumé for the piles of scholarship applications I knew I'd be filling out in a few short years.

I was a typical scholarship kid: smart, competitive, poor, and terrified. At fourteen, I was not savvy enough to understand that loans and need-based grants were in place to help cover what scholarships and part-time jobs could not. I earnestly believed that college was an all-or-nothing pursuit in which I would either prove myself enough to be let in the door or fail miserably and be shut out forever.

My plan, though it may have cost me some sleepless nights, ultimately worked. I got into Knox College, a well-respected private liberal arts college of only 1,200 students, just an hour's drive from my parents. At the time, Knox's tuition was one of the highest in Illinois, but it had a strong financial aid program. Despite this and the college's supportive atmosphere, though, I regularly felt out of place on campus.

The stately brick buildings and pages-long syllabi were less terrifying than my sophisticated, well-read, and well-traveled classmates. Their conversations about traveling to places like Prague and Barcelona were over my head (I had never been on an airplane), and they couldn't understand why I was so fascinated with the TVs in the dorm's common areas (it was the first time in my life I had cable).

Trying to find people to belong to, I again selfishly turned to community service. I joined Alpha Phi Omega (APO), a co-ed service fraternity that was active at Knox and welcomed anyone who was interested. My time with APO allowed me to get off Knox's beautiful but insulated campus and spend time with other students and community members. I would discover that many of the students in APO, like me, squirmed uncomfortably when their peers used the word "townies" to describe people who looked an awful lot like their parents, siblings, friends, and neighbors from back home.

After graduating with honors from Knox in four years, I went directly to graduate school. On the surface, then, my path through the education system appeared as smooth and typical as they come, with few bumps and no real detours along the way: high school straight to a traditional four-year college, and then straight to graduate school. Most of my problems were either internal—that same "imposter syndrome" that I feel occasionally even today—or had to do with figuring out how to finance my education. I used community service to deal with both.

It wasn't until my time at Purdue that I realized community work could help me address my problems and work through my class identity in a different way. Before Purdue, community service had helped me to pay for my education by making me an impressive scholarship applicant and had helped me meet other students who, like me, sometimes felt more comfortable off campus than on.

At Purdue, several positive experiences on and off campus afforded the perfect opportunity to consider how my class identity could actually contribute to my sense of who I was, both as an academic and as a person. On campus, I worked with several professors and peers who shared my interest in community-based work, public rhetoric, and class identity. Off campus, my part-time work in local restaurants provided me real connections in the area beyond the university.

When I first stumbled into Maize, the downtown Lafayette restaurant where I worked for nearly all of my time at Purdue, I was desperate for extra income and had just interviewed with a telemarketing company. As luck would have it, the restaurant owner was sitting at the bar happily drinking an afternoon gin and tonic when I walked in. He asked me if I had any experience waiting tables, and when I answered that I did, he bellowed, "Alright! Let's get you a job!"

With its starched white tablecloths and mahogany bar, Maize was probably the fanciest restaurant I had ever seen up close. I knew that teaching assistants were not supposed to work outside of the department, but I also knew those heavy leather menus and sparkling wine glasses meant that this place could be the difference between taking out more student loans and surviving on my own. For me, it was an easy choice.

I was proud of my restaurant work—proud that I was good at the work itself, proud that I could manage a part-time job in addition to my doctoral studies, and mostly, proud that I got along well with my interesting, intelligent co-workers who other Purdue students may have cast aside as "townies." My work in restaurants gave me a sense of connection to the community and a sense of pride in my background, both of which indirectly furthered my interest in community engagement.

On a more practical level, I also knew more people in the community because of my work in restaurants; in fact, I first encountered one of our community partners while working a lunch shift. During that shift, as I was making another pot of coffee for a table of well-dressed men working over lunch, a large group of fifteen to twenty began trickling in. My manager knew the group was coming and had prepared for them by setting up a long table along the back wall, where we typically put our largest groups. Two experienced servers would serve the table; as a relative newcomer, I was relegated to serving the pairs and tables of three or four that I could handle.

When I found out that the large group was with the Lafayette Adult Resource Academy, I was interested immediately because of my service background. My interest was intensified by how much they contrasted with the restaurant's usual lunch crowd. There were no confident men in suits or perfumed women carrying large designer purses or even young college students in Abercrombie and Fitch sweaters and cords. Everyone in the group was dressed casually in jeans and T-shirts from discount stores. Many of them looked nervous, and some even looked obviously uncomfortable. When I got a spare moment, I asked my co-workers about the group.

My manager explained that the LARA group was at Maize to practice dining skills for "business and interview situations." The group's teachers, the two middle-aged women who had led everyone else into the restaurant, had called my manager the previous week and explained that everything needed to go perfectly so that the students could focus on practicing their dining skills. The teachers had chosen Maize because it was a nice restaurant suited to interviews and business lunches and because it was downtown, relatively close, at the time, to LARA's building.

After my manager explained the situation to me, I was entranced. I had shuffled through college and my early years of graduate school feeling regularly out of place, not in the classroom, but in nearly every other situation. I didn't know how to use chopsticks, I *still* had never been on an airplane, and I just plain didn't get Wes Anderson's movies. When a grad school buddy asked where I had traveled, my cheeks burned red when she and others laughed at my honest response. "I went to Florida once," I had said. I learned quickly that this wasn't the right answer.

On the one hand, I was as in-place as a person could be at Purdue: I was white, Midwestern, a young "traditional" student who had gone straight from high school to college to grad school. On the other, there always seemed to be something that I didn't understand, some joke I didn't get, or some way of behaving that I couldn't mimic. As I watched the LARA students order lunch and make practiced conversations, I wished a similar event existed for PhD students who felt unsure how to act during conference lunches or coffee with their professors or even drinks with their sophisticated peers.

Despite my working-class upbringing or work in the service industry, I was undeniably in a position of privilege over most of the LARA students dining at Maize that day. These people were struggling to pass the GED test and gain entry-level employment, and the irony that many of them would have happily traded places with the people serving them lunch was not lost on me or the other servers.

During this moment, as with many of the moments when I ventured off Purdue's campus, I came face-to-face with the complicated identities and privileges that defined my time as a graduate student. Just like the LARA students, I had to learn certain class-coded behaviors to be successful. These behaviors were subtle, unstated, and ever shifting, a combination that made perceiving and learning them nearly impossible.

Just like the LARA students, I was struggling to make ends meet, as evidenced by the second job I had taken at Maize to supplement my income as a teaching assistant. And even with that second job, I often struggled to pay the bills. The difference between the LARA students and me was that I could have quit my PhD program and used my college degree to gain professional employment; the LARA students did not have that option.

This day at Maize was my first encounter with LARA, the adult literacy program that would be one of the community partners for the three-year engagement project that formed the core of my dissertation. I am tempted to pretend that I realized in that moment, in my first year as a graduate student, that the program would make a fantastic partner for community engagement and that further, developing and researching an engagement project was exactly what I wanted to do for my dissertation.

Any reader would easily sniff out that fib. The processes of developing dissertation topics or identifying community partners are rarely (if ever) so neat. Still, witnessing the business lunch lesson kick-started my interest in LARA and offered a good metaphor for what I ultimately wanted to do at Purdue: get off campus to see what was going on and how I could get involved.

Allen

My earliest memories of civic responsibility emerge from my experiences with the Cub Scouts. Often, we performed civic duties to earn merit badges for lessons like learning American history and government, and of course, for "doing good deeds." As an adult, it's strange now reading about the ideas underpinning the activities we completed, noticing connections between them and the *praxis*-oriented approach that frames much of my current work. For example, the scouting approach of "learning by doing" mirrors my *praxis* methodology that is influenced by ancient rhetoric and that helps guide my service-learning classes.

My parents were wise to enroll me in scouts because my early lessons in civic engagement probably influenced my long-term education more so than my high-school experiences. My time at Hayfield Junior High and High School in Fairfax County, Virginia, in many ways, taught me what *not* to do with my future students rather than preparing me for college. My problems with authority and rambunctious personality didn't fit well with my football coach-history teachers, who were also football coaches, and before long, I was skipping school at the nearby 7–11 convenience store and getting into fights.

By this point in life, my scouting days were long behind me, and my education consisted of unsuccessful stints in summer classes, and eventually, a second high school, Robert E. Lee. My experience at Lee High School was marginally better, but before long, I was in trouble again for truancy (Springfield Mall was right across the street), and a career in music seemed more exciting than four years in college.

So when a school administrator said, "We think it's best if you not return to Lee next year," I agreed and never went back. So despite having every opportunity to succeed in my middle-class upbringing, the mix of my immaturity and one-size-fits-all public education led me to Bryant Adult Education Center. Now called Bryant Alternative High School, it is similar in many ways to LARA, one of our community partners in Lafayette, Indiana.

Quite simply, Bryant saved me from becoming a high-school dropout. After knocking my head against a traditional high-school system I found unfair and inflexible, Bryant provided the individual attention and freedom that I needed to succeed. Interestingly, though I graduated from Bryant, my diploma actually reads "Thomas A. Edison High School," a *third* high school in northern Virginia.

When I asked my English teacher at Bryant about the name change, she explained, "They do that so people won't discriminate against you. Employers might not hire you if they see that you went to Bryant. They'll think you're a white trash loser." Although I had finally achieved my goal of graduating from high school, my education was overshadowed by the source of my salvation, an adult education center for near-miss dropouts. Though Bryant offered a fully accredited diploma, many people considered it a last chance dump for losers and troubled teens.

After looking back at our yearbook—students' pictures were taped to pages because Bryant couldn't afford glossy prints—I can see why this was the case. My twenty or so classmates were an unlikely mix of head bangers, hippies, and hip-hop wannabes. I recall vividly my first day at Bryant, sitting in a waiting room filled with a hodgepodge of castaway furniture from other high schools. It had been a stressful week, and I was waiting for my scores from the GED pretest. After leaving my second high school, Robert E. Lee, my mother had said "Take the GED so you can at least go to community college."

After band practice (I was going to make it big in heavy metal), I swung by Bryant to take the GED pretest. I sat in the waiting room with the ripped chairs and wobbly tables, along with the other "nontraditional" students. Some of them struggled with their squirming kids, some listened to their blaring Walkmans, while others, like me, sat looking awkward in what we hoped would be our last encounter with public education.

While I glanced around, I felt a sharp pain on my right ear. I flinched and swept my hand at what I thought was a bee. My hand hit the fingers of a short, burly man in a button-down shirt; he was one of Bryant's guidance counselors.

In a gruff voice he said, "Get up and come into my office. We need to talk." Given his painful grip on my ear, I had no choice but to stand and follow. Still holding my ear between his fingers, he sat me down and slammed the door.

"What the hell is your problem?" he barked. Stunned, I replied "What? What do you mean what the hell is my problem? I don't have a problem. What's *your* problem? Why did you grab my ear? That hurt!"

"You *do* have a problem. Your problem is *you*. And I grabbed your ear to get your attention. Someone needs to get your attention. You're screwing up your education, and you're about to screw up your life. How many credits do you need to graduate?" he asked.

"Um, I don't know. And why do you ask? I'm not here to finish high school. I'm here to take the GED so I can get on with my life," I said.

He laughed and replied, "No, you're not. Do you know what you scored on that pretest? I'll tell you. You scored too damn high to take the GED. You need to finish high school, and you're going to do it here, at Bryant." I stared at him as he tapped away on his (metal) computer searching for my high-school records.

That adult education counselor, who still works at Bryant, drastically changed my life by grabbing my ear and pushing me to reconsider the direction of my education and my life. He definitely got my attention, and by the end of our meeting, I was registered at Bryant and on my way to completing my high-school diploma.

Following Bryant, and a few more failed attempts at heavy metal stardom, I had a short-lived career driving a truck and working in a warehouse. Eventually, I learned the hard way through persistent back problems and dodgy salaries that I would have to continue my education, and that meant enrolling at northern Virginia Community College (NOVA).

At NOVA, I took my first writing classes and even tutored in the writing center at the suggestion of my first-year writing professor, Dorothy Seyler (author of *Read, Reason, Write* and other composition books). At first,

I helped pay my way at NOVA by working as a summer-hire office flunky in the Department of Defense at Ft. Belvoir, Virginia. But as my writing skills improved, I began helping administrative assistants and engineers with professional communication.

After two years at NOVA, I earned my associate's degree and transferred to Virginia Tech (VT). Like Jaclyn, I felt out of place in college. Though I was among other students from northern Virginia, I was twenty-eight, much older than most of my peers. All in all, though I had worked hard to capitalize on the state's second-chance education system, I was still the awkward, nontraditional student in every class.

However, during my time at VT while studying with Jim Dubinsky, I was able to combine my Cub Scout civic experiences with my academic efforts in a productive and meaningful way. My original plan was to finish my bachelor's and then return to the Washington, DC, area to continue my work as a technical writer for the government or work in the private sector. But after studying with Jim, who showed me that writing could serve many purposes, I found that my path was taking a different direction, a direction that included writing centers and service-learning.

Building on my experience tutoring in the NOVA writing center, I began working in the writing center at VT. I took more professional writing courses, which led me to my first service-learning project. This project involved collaborating with the town of Christiansburg, Virginia, to create their first newsletter. I stayed at VT for my master's, and my service-learning experience there helped me work as a technical writer and adjunct instructor in the DC area before I realized I would have to obtain a PhD. My positive experiences with service-learning at VT also led to my interest in public rhetoric and civic engagement in the PhD program at Purdue.

Once at Purdue, I didn't really think about Bryant. After all, I had worked as a technical writer for the federal government, had a master's degree, and had taught writing courses at respected institutions; I didn't have to prove myself at Purdue. My past in adult education was sort of a dark mystery that I didn't like to talk about, though I didn't avoid it if asked. As Jaclyn noted above, many graduate students already feel like imposters; imagine if too many people found out about Bryant!

My past might have remained hidden had it not been for LARA and its downtown Lafayette location near the South Street Bridge that crosses the Wabash River. One day as I drove home from class, I crossed the bridge and noticed LARA's sign. The sign barely registered in my mind the first few times I saw it. But slowly my curiosity grew, and I began squinting as I passed it so that I could read the smaller black letters under the large L-A-R-A. The letters read, "Lafayette Adult Resource Academy." That's when I made the connection between LARA and Bryant, between my present and my past.

I thought to myself, "I bet LARA is like Bryant." Day after day, when I crossed the bridge, I looked over at the LARA sign and remembered my time at Bryant and its influence on my position as a PhD student at Purdue. I certainly could have begun my collegiate process by enrolling at NOVA with a GED. But had the counselor at Bryant allowed me to take the GED test, I'm sure that my path through community college, challenging enough already, would have been far more difficult, and might not have happened at all. So I like to credit Bryant with fundamentally changing my life, and that is one of the reasons I felt so connected to LARA.

FINDING A COMMUNITY PARTNER

The personal vignettes in the previous sections are intended to show that the authors shared an orientation toward the university and the community, even though their backgrounds differ. The authors' dedication to service and local needs, as well as their reluctance to limit their work to the academy's narrow confines, shaped the CWEST tremendously, even from its earliest stages. The particular university and community circumstances the authors observed also shaped the project; the distance between Purdue and Lafayette, discussed in earlier sections, was particularly important.

Reading more scholarship and having more discussions reinforced for the authors that their observations were not unique to the Purdue-Lafayette community. The commonplace distance between universities and communities supports the idea that community engagement should be informed by research. When projects include research, findings not only inform a particular project, but can also help others develop community-based work that addresses university-community boundaries in their own local contexts.

Numerous scholars describe such boundaries. In the frequently cited article, "The Rhetorician as an Agent of Social Change," Ellen Cushman (1996) discusses the distance between Rensselaer Polytechnic Institute (RPI) and Troy, New York. She describes the Approach, a large staircase that serves as an entrance into the university. The monument, originally given to the university by the city, had fallen into disrepair at the time of Cushman's writing, and she uses it, as she does the geography of Troy and RPI, to symbolize the community and university's strained relationship.

Several states away, eerily similar geography and landmarks reveal the distance between Purdue and Lafayette. Just west of the Wabash River, Purdue's immense campus and related businesses sprawl outward toward the cornfields, while just east across the river, downtown Lafayette has developed in more modest ways. Nevertheless, local marketing campaigns and publications depict the two towns as one, connected by a footbridge that runs over the Wabash River bringing Purdue's bell tower and Lafayette's courthouse together. The image has even made its way into a large mural at a local restaurant.

The footbridge over the Wabash has not fallen into disrepair like the Approach at RPI, but the landmarks share a common characteristic. For both, the reality of the university-community relationship is far more complicated than the landmarks' metaphors of connection would suggest. In a sense, both landmarks have been asked to do too much: The distance between the university and community is simply too great to repair with a bridge or a staircase.

As with RPI and Troy, the geographic split has made its way into the local language about the Purdue-Lafayette area. Purdue students and Lafayette citizens alike talk about venturing "over the river," a phrase well understood in the local context. Among Purdue undergraduates, going over the river for a night out means leaving the college bars that fill the west side and hanging out in the "dives" with the "locals" or "townies." Among Lafayette citizens, going over the river essentially means going into Boilermaker territory.

Of course, differences between the two sides of the river move beyond stereotypes to actual differences in resources and experiences. Most locals know, for example, that the public schools over the river in West Lafayette perform much better than those in Lafayette. For the authors, the severity of this difference came into focus during the meeting of Patricia Sullivan's public rhetoric course discussed earlier in the chapter, with a course reading about the graduation rates of the two largest local high schools.

These statistics (65 percent graduation rate for Lafayette's Jefferson High School vs. 95.4 percent for West Lafayette High School) suggested the need for building a better relationship between the two sides of the river and using Purdue's resources to support local education (Indiana Department of Education, 2009). The specific nature of the statistics shaped the authors' ideas for how to engage the community. Specifically, important questions arose that guided the project from its inception: If 35 percent of Jeff High students were not graduating, where were they going? Further, could a university-community partnership help?

Some nongraduates were going to what Mike Rose labels "second-chance institutions" in *Back to School: Why Everyone Deserves a Second Chance at Education*. Rose published *Back to School* in 2012, five years after the CWEST project began. Rose's book provides both validation for a project like the CWEST and possible critique (or at least a complication) of Jaclyn and Allen's experiences as university students and researchers.

Rose argues that too much education scholarship has focused on elite institutions and research universities, such as Purdue, where students like the authors spent most of their time sheltered in brick buildings amid reasonably up-to-date technology and impressive library collections. Focusing on the traditional educational path, Rose argues, creates many problems, among them the collective failure to realize that the label "traditional student" has become increasingly flawed as more students, like Allen, pursue alternative paths.

By stubbornly continuing to focus on that traditional route, even as it may no longer be "tradition," Rose (2012) argues, researchers ignore the experiences of many students, including those who perhaps most need them to research, theorize, and change our flawed education system. Rose raises many important questions, including, "How adequate are the programs we have in place to remedy the failures of K-12 education?" (p. 181). In Lafayette, Jefferson High School's 35 percent dropout rate in 2005 would surely constitute one such failure.

Locally, the primary resource to remedy this failure, to use Rose's (2012) language, is LARA, a free adult education organization that offers programs in GED preparation, family literacy, job skills training, and English as a Second Language (ESL). LARA is aligned locally with WorkOne, Indiana's employment program that helps people prepare for and find work, as well as register for unemployment services. The programs share a building, some staff, and a reciprocal relationship. Some students just go to LARA to prepare for the GED or just go to WorkOne to use job databases, but many use both the programs.

In some ways, Rose's (2012) question about the adequacy of second-chance programs validates the authors' efforts. LARA and WorkOne certainly constitute such programs, and the authors sought to learn more about them and adult education broadly through mixed methods, participatory research. On the other hand, the authors clearly benefited from the focus on "traditional" experiences in education research and therefore held a position of privilege in the community. To collaborate successfully with LARA and WorkOne, it was necessary to understand and examine this privilege.

The beginning of this chapter promises to tell the whole story of the community engagement project, including the messy parts of the process. The authors could not deliver on this promise by pretending that the story went as follows. First, discover the poor graduation rates of Lafayette's largest high school; second, become motivated to contribute to programs that helped students who had dropped out; and third, approach LARA and WorkOne, the area's primary programs for such work.

The reality was far less linear than such a story would suggest, but in essence, Jaclyn and Allen felt motivated by the statistics shared in the public rhetoric class to contribute to local "nontraditional" education like LARA and WorkOne. However, a collaboration with LARA and WorkOne was not predetermined. As shared in chapter 2, the authors' professor, Patricia Sullivan, emphasized the importance of first determining the needs of the community and their willingness to collaborate before beginning the early steps of a civic engagement project.

Allen and Jaclyn were interested in adult literacy because of their past, and they had some data and basic information about the local situation. However, this kind of basic information is not enough to begin a partnership with the community. To begin a project, much more information is required, information about the community's needs, values, and interest in collaborating. To gather this information, both meeting with community partners and learning more about the local context are necessary.

When they began meeting with the community members, the authors had one general question in mind: What, beyond an interest and willingness to help, could they (and Purdue in general) offer to organizations like LARA and WorkOne and to local adult education? With one look at LARA's website and some Internet research, one possible answer emerged: the Purdue OWL and Jaclyn and Allen's expertise, as Writing Lab and OWL staff, in designing and delivering online instructional resources.

Additional research on Web-based adult literacy resources supported this possible answer, as it quickly became clear that such resources were sorely lacking. In early 2007, when the CWEST project was in its earliest stages, virtually no free online resources existed for adult education. A search for GED preparation resources, for example, yielded only one deeply buried website with a description of the exam and a handful of sample questions. Most online resources for job hunters, including the sample résumés and cover letters on the Purdue OWL, assumed a college education.

Further, LARA's clunky website served an informational rather than instructional purpose, with only information about the program instead of educational materials that teachers or students could use. Coincidentally, the website had been developed by Purdue service-learning students, a reality that proved the authors' suspicions that such projects were not always a "magic pill" for community organizations. Moreover, only seconds spent on the Indiana's employment sites made it clear that usable, entry-level job resources were sorely needed.

The authors' own potential contributions to LARA, WorkOne, and local adult education constituted only half of the equation, since what was desired was a partnership that would be truly collaborative, reciprocal, and sustainable. Asking what the university partners could contribute to a collaboration, then, was only half of the question. The other half was, what could the community partners contribute?

LARA and WorkOne, two programs with longstanding roles in the community, had the potential for working with a community partner over a span of time. To an engagement project, the programs could offer a wealth of expertise about areas like adult literacy pedagogy, GED preparation, ESL instruction, and even the local job hunt. Further, the programs' long history in the community supported their chances of being around well into the future, which could contribute to a collaboration's potential to stick around as well.

Despite LARA's and WorkOne's longstanding role and influence in the community, their spaces suggest their vulnerability and even transience. At the CWEST's early stages in 2007, the programs had recently moved from the old Loeb Building in downtown Lafayette (which displayed the sign visible from South Street Bridge) to the former Washington Elementary School on the city's north side in an area designated as an "Urban Enterprise Zone" (this designation basically means the area is socioeconomically challenged).

The area surrounding LARA/WorkOne is of lower income, with rundown houses that often host drug dealers. The new location was a step up in terms of space and convenience, with a stop on the bus line, a large parking lot, and a playground that students' children could use. However, that the programs relocated into a building with a previous purpose, as opposed to one built specifically for them, speaks volumes about their resources and role in the community.

LARA's and WorkOne's relocation into a former school building, a physical castoff of the local school system, contrasts greatly with the care and expense poured into much of Purdue's planning. Purdue's meticulously planned campus includes the spaces in which the authors studied and worked regularly during their time at Purdue, which again speaks to their privilege as university participants. The development of Academy Park, a five-acre space in the center of Purdue's campus, perhaps best signifies such care and expense.

The meticulously planned and beautifully landscaped Academy Park developed in the 1990s contains pedestrian walkways and green spaces for performances and outdoor class meetings. Inspired by Plato's Academy, Purdue's Academy Park showcases large stones inscribed with words from Plato, Aristotle, and Socrates. Among the words is a quote from Diogenes: "The foundation of any state is the education of its youth."

Despite the meticulous planning applied to Academy Park, the meaning of this particular quote within the context of the Park seems unclear. One could reasonably ask what "youth" the planners had in mind: Purdue students? Or the youth of Indiana, including those "across the river" in Lafayette?

From their view in Heavilon Hall, home to the Purdue Writing Lab and one of the buildings surrounding Academy Park, Jaclyn and Allen optimistically hoped that the university's answer was the latter. And if it wasn't, the authors hoped to do their part to extend the university's mission to the larger community rather than centering intellectual activity solely on campus.

THE RESEARCHER'S ROLES IN THE PROJECT

To help explain some contextual information, this section provides an overview of the authors' roles at the beginning of the CWEST project. This information is intended to set up the next chapter, which includes a broader description of the planning and early stages of the project.

As discussed previously, Allen and Jaclyn were both graduate students in Purdue's PhD program in rhetoric and composition. Jaclyn was focusing on writing program administration while Allen was taking the professional writing track. At the beginning stages of the CWEST, Allen and Jaclyn were juggling full-time graduate course schedules and preparing for preliminary exams (or comps). As teaching assistants (TAs), both had taught first-year and professional writing. Both were tutoring in the Writing Lab, an experience that clearly contributed to the CWEST project.

Beyond these fairly common graduate school responsibilities, Jaclyn and Allen both held graduate administrative positions—Jaclyn worked as the Writing Lab's workshop coordinator and later as a teaching mentor in the composition program, and Allen held the OWL coordinator position. So to say that the authors were graduate students during the CWEST project is too simple a statement. Both authors were students, tutors, and emerging administrators.

The CWEST developed from Patricia Sullivan's public rhetorics course and took root in Linda Bergmann's Writing Lab. As Allen and Jaclyn had both been working with Linda in the lab, early conversations about the CWEST came easily. The project, Linda said, had come along at a good time because she had been thinking about ways the lab and the OWL might extend their land-grant state university obligations.

More specifically, Linda saw the CWEST as a great way to build on some of the lab's existing community engagement efforts. These efforts included the Tecumseh Junior High School Annual Essay Contest (which lab staff members and tutors judged); the WiderNet Project with the University of Iowa; and the local creative writing initiative, Words on the Go. The CWEST would be different, however, in that it would be participatory and empirical in its approach.

Despite the initial enthusiasm, Linda, like Patricia Sullivan, emphasized the importance of determining the needs and willingness of LARA and WorkOne before the project began. Importantly, however, all of the key players at Purdue shared a similar vision of the CWEST. As an overview of the model that emerged from the CWEST and that contributed to this shared vision, the next section presents the methodology.

EMERGENT METHODOLOGY

From the maps, stages, and timelines included in coming chapters, readers might conclude that everything was figured out and organized from the earliest days of the project. But as the book will show, this was far from the truth. From scholarship, good mentorship, and combined personal experiences, Allen and Jaclyn had some solid guiding principles. But much of the methodology that emerged from the CWEST occurred organically as all partners stumbled along. Still, figure 1.1 may help readers understand the general methodology that emerged from the project.

The beginning sections of subsequent chapters return to this graphic to help readers contextualize information in each chapter. Also, readers may reference the generative questions in the appendix that correspond with each chapter to help their own work. Again, the goal is not to provide a neat or linear version of how the CWEST project played out; instead, the hope is that these

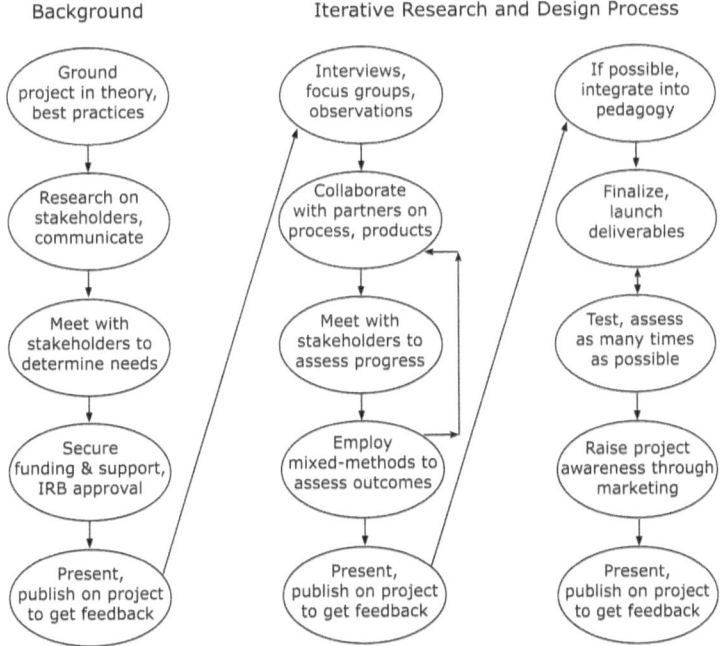

Figure 1.1   Emergent CWEST Methodology

graphics and questions will help illustrate what the project involved, with the understanding that the overall process was far more messy and complex than any graph, timeline, or simple set of questions could show.

As the process began, the authors familiarized themselves with theories of civic discourse and engagement, some of which have been mentioned in this chapter and some of which will be discussed in the remaining chapters as they relate to subject matter in the book. For the next step, the authors carefully studied the project's stakeholders and collaborated closely with LARA and WorkOne, as well as the Purdue partners, to determine needs.

Securing funding came next, as did securing IRB approval, since empirical research with human participants played an important role in the project. The next steps formed the development, design, and test stages of the CWEST, which followed an iterative design process. As the project progressed, the authors presented the project at writing center and composition conferences and submitted work with Linda Bergmann for publication.[1] Last came launching, retesting, and marketing the CWEST project locally through press releases and even pencils printed with the CWEST URL.

Jaclyn and Allen's current work as faculty members shows that the model presented here is flexible (see chapter 6). Allen, for example, completed service-learning at his institution for nearly two years before seeking funding and IRB approval for community-based research. Jaclyn, on the other hand, received funding to develop service-learning curricula before she decided what specific projects to complete.

Still, the authors' recent work is guided by the theory, empiricism, and iterative design process from the CWEST, even while they have diverged from the model shown at figure 1.1. They argue that even though others' work might not look exactly like the CWEST, activist researchers and writing center administrators can follow the project's process to build and sustain their own university-community relationships.

NOTE

1. See "The Engaged Dissertation: Three Points of View," in *Collaborative Futures: Critical Reflections on Publicly Active Graduate Education* (2012).

Chapter 2

Community Partners and Overview of Research Methods

This chapter describes the authors' early collaboration with LARA and WorkOne. Shared here are the strategies used to contact the organizations; negotiate the needs of community and university partners; communicate project goals with diverse stakeholders; and obtain approval and support for the project from the Purdue IRB and granting organizations at Purdue.

Writing for a variety of aims and audiences formed a central part of this work: Jaclyn and Allen wrote to introduce themselves and their ideas, to communicate and formalize project goals, and to obtain approval and support. This chapter details the process of composing many of these documents and provides the general information about LARA and WorkOne obtained from early communication and research. The discussion in this chapter covers the next four steps of the emergent methodology, as outlined by the model in chapter 1 (see figure 2.1).

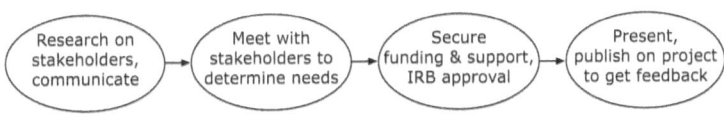

Figure 2.1 Initial Research and Funding Steps

Chapter 2

REACHING OUT TO THE COMMUNITY

Just like any talk between good friends, Allen and Jaclyn's conversations about the project happened easily and enthusiastically. Graduate school is filled with these types of conversations: at Purdue, the coffee shops, graduate labs and lounges, and libraries often buzz with the excitement of students exchanging ideas and starting new projects. The authors knew that these conversations over coffee would be the easy part. The next steps, communicating with the potential community partners and venturing off the familiar landscape of campus, would present the greater challenge.

This work began, as it does for many graduate students, with conversations with trusted mentors, in this specific case, Linda Bergmann, the director of Purdue's Writing Lab, and Patricia Sullivan, the graduate director and professor of the public rhetorics course where the project began. Two of Bergmann and Sullivan's recommendations most influenced initial contact with LARA and WorkOne: first, understand the potential stakeholders, and second, go into the community.

First, Bergmann and Sullivan both suggested mapping out all of the project's potential stakeholders when considering how to communicate with them about the work. The first map, shown in figure 2.2, illustrates some of the geographic, educational, and community elements Jaclyn and Allen perceived as influencing a collaboration with LARA/WorkOne. These maps

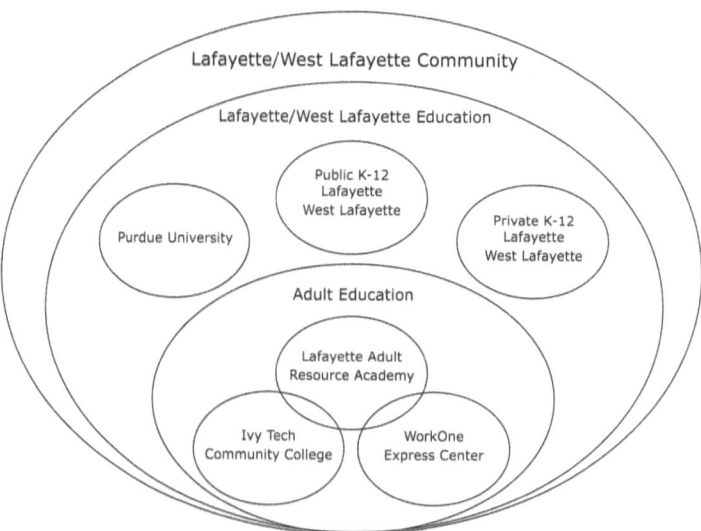

Figure 2.2 CWEST Project Map 1

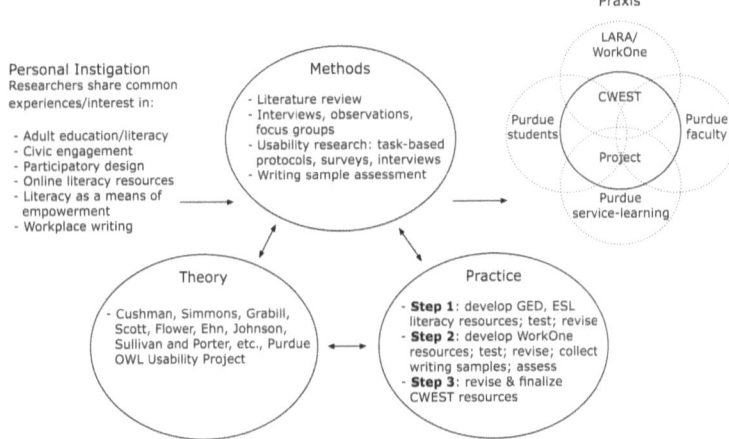

Figure 2.3   CWEST Project Map 2

illustrate how the project attempted to bring together many disparate ideas, theories, methods, stakeholders, and institutions.

The second map, shown in figure 2.3 and adapted from Sullivan and Porter's (1997) *Opening Spaces*, illustrates a number of different elements involved in the authors' vision of the CWEST. It shows their personal instigation (also see chapter 1), theories, research methods, and planned practices, as well as a graphical display of the intended collaboration between stakeholders.

Both maps emphasize that the *university* partners need to go to the community, both physically and philosophically. This, then, was Linda's and Patricia's second recommendation: go *into* the community. Meeting the community on their ground sends a clear message, one of respect for the staff members' time and respect for their willingness to possibly collaborate with the university. In an early conversation about the project, Patricia said "You have to go into the community to learn more about your potential partners. You have to learn about their *needs*. This has to be a *needs-based* project."

With Patricia's advice in mind, Jaclyn and Allen conducted initial research on local organizations—including LARA and WorkOne—that connected to local literacy and education in the ways illustrated in the maps shown in figures 2.2 and 2.3. Next, the authors reached out to LARA in a simple email to the program's assistant director, Suzanne.[1] At this point, the specific outcomes or goals for a partnership with LARA and WorkOne were open ended.

Allen and Jaclyn believed, however, that the Purdue OWL might play a role in the project, and they hoped that the project might fill the OWL's gap in adult literacy resources. The email to Suzanne kept things open and simple. It introduced Jaclyn and Allen as Purdue graduate students who wished to learn more about LARA and WorkOne and explore the possibility of a partnership between the two organizations and Purdue's Writing Lab.

Suzanne returned the email quickly. Still, a week between that initial email and the first meeting with her allowed plenty of time for enthusiasm and nervousness to build. When the meeting actually occurred, the authors had not forgotten all of the readings and discussions about service projects that overstate their own importance; university participants who view themselves as rescuing the community; or popular media's caricatures of community projects, all seemingly life changing, effortless, and devoid of human tensions. They had not forgotten.

But, in that week of anticipation, the authors had unwittingly placed those messages on the backburner and traded them for feelings of eagerness for what the *university* could do for the community. This led to a somewhat anticlimactic first meeting, despite all the mapping and preparation described in this and the previous chapter. When the meeting with Suzanne occurred, Allen and Jaclyn practically floated into the LARA/WorkOne building, no doubt just like previous Purdue students and faculty before them.

During a brief tour, Suzanne showed off LARA's main learning lab, WorkOne's computer room, a small gym with donated day-old bagels from the local Panera, and hallways decorated with staff pictures and advertisements for local educational and social programs. After the tour, Jaclyn, Allen, and Suzanne sat down in Suzanne's office. It was during this sit-down that the authors realized how one sided their enthusiasm might have been. Though Suzanne was polite and pleasant, her reserve immediately showed. It became clear that she had been in this meeting before.

LARA and WorkOne may never have partnered with the Purdue Writing Lab, but both programs had worked with other undergraduate and graduate students, all of them, no doubt, as enthusiastic and well intentioned as Allen and Jaclyn. One part of the meeting did get Suzanne's attention, though: mention of the Purdue OWL. When she learned that Jaclyn had developed content for the OWL, that Allen served as OWL coordinator, and that both were interested in involving the OWL in the possible project, Suzanne grew more interested. She even said that she and the other teachers at LARA used the OWL regularly with students.

This news presented a minor conflict. On the one hand, that the teachers used the Purdue OWL's existing resources somewhat diminished the authors' hypothesis that adult basic education (ABE) organizations like LARA and WorkOne may want OWL resources that were tailored to the needs of their students. On the other hand, Suzanne showed a clear interest in the OWL that made her more receptive to a potential collaboration. Where she had seemed initially reserved, she seemed excited about working together to create something new and valuable for the OWL and for LARA.

Suzanne's interest in the OWL supports the need for engagement with clear and desired benefits for the community. As Sura and Leon (2013) argue in "We Don't Need Any More Brochures: Rethinking Deliverables in Service-Learning Curricula," deliverables alone do not ensure a useful project: such deliverables must also reflect community needs. Suzanne may have initially hesitated to collaborate because she had experienced service projects that produced disappointing results, such as LARA's poorly designed website that was created in a service-learning course.

Suzanne's interest in the Purdue OWL affirmed some of the initial ideas about the CWEST project's focus. After the meeting, Allen and Jaclyn felt sure that the project should focus on creating new OWL resources in the area of ABE. Suzanne had seemed receptive to this idea during the meeting and admitted that some resources would be better if they were tailored to her students' needs.

GED resources provide perhaps the clearest example of what the OWL lacked. The GED test contained a forty-five-minute essay[2] that resembled timed writings on other standardized tests. Before the CWEST project, the OWL did not contain resources on writing any timed essays. This may reflect teaching preferences: few teachers of writing *enjoy* teaching timed writing, and OWL content is produced and updated by writing teachers and tutors. At LARA and similar programs, however, instructors cannot ignore timed writing instruction, since many of their students are working to pass the GED.

The GED exam provides a fantastic example of the exchange of expertise that a prospective project would require. Creating GED resources would require the adult education expertise offered by LARA teachers, and designing the resources for the OWL would require Allen and Jaclyn's time and expertise in online content development. This attitude change brought everyone closer to the reciprocal approach that the authors repeatedly discussed from the project's beginning but could not truly envision before crossing the bridge into Lafayette and sitting down with the prospective community partner.

The next step was to formalize this thinking with a proposal. The authors hoped that offering a more formal outline of the project would help build a stronger relationship between the partners by making the work transparent, preventing some of the disappointing results that the community partner had experienced in the past, and inviting dialogue and feedback. To begin the proposal, the authors returned to their mentors, Linda and Patricia, who both reiterated that they should consider and tailor the communication to the project's various stakeholders.

LEARNING MORE ABOUT THE COMMUNITY PARTNERS

The information in this section reflects the authors' earliest findings about LARA and WorkOne. This information is less empirical than data in subsequent chapters, but it is important nonetheless. Jaclyn and Allen learned much about LARA and WorkOne, for example, during the tour of the building with Suzanne, as well as during the first staff meeting that they attended. This section provides a sense of the programs' histories, missions, strategies, funding and other resources, and roles in the community. It also illustrates the type of contextual information activist scholars should develop in the early stages of their university-community work.

The Lafayette Adult Resource Academy (LARA)

LARA is located only a few miles from Purdue's campus, but the two seem a world apart. LARA sits on Union Street, a busy road that intersects with Lafayette's downtown district and its major highway. The former grade school building that houses LARA is surrounded on three sides by rows of houses, many of which are as rundown as the old, rusted cars parked in their driveways. The fourth side of the building faces a local bar and a nonprofit thrift store. Hopscotch boards decorate one corner of the parking lot, and the small yard surrounding the lot contains playground equipment.

Before moving to its current location, LARA was located about a mile away in a similar neighborhood in downtown Lafayette. The program's location changes are only one part of its history of change, a history that also includes regular shifts in leadership, funding, and name. The program's history illustrates how LARA's mission and role in the community have been influenced by changes to its funding, leadership, and relationship with other programs.

From its inception, the academy[3] was the result of collaboration among community leaders, Purdue faculty, state and federal government, and local programs. LARA officially began in 1976, when Purdue education professor Alden Moe proposed to the United States Office of Education's Right to Read Initiative. The community was awarded $50,000 to establish an adult literacy program called a "Reading Academy" (LARA website). The Young Women's Christian Association (YWCA) of Greater Lafayette became the program's fiscal agent, donated a large space, and inaugurated the YWCA Reading Academy that same year.

A couple of years after the academy's founding, the director added state funding to federal and local support by applying for and receiving ABE money from the state of Indiana. This new funding clearly expanded support for the academy. Additionally, the new funding required that the program conduct a formal assessment of community needs.

With the help of two Purdue research assistants, Professor Moe led this assessment. He used interviews, questionnaires, and study of the area's demographics, geography, economy, and opportunities for education and culture to investigate community needs. Assessment findings suggested that the community needed resources for ABE, GED preparation, and ESL. The academy responded by refining its program objectives around these three areas.

In 1979, the academy's name was officially changed from the YWCA Reading Academy to the Lafayette Adult Reading Academy when the Lafayette School Corporation (LSC) incorporated the program and took control of its state funding (LARA website). The YWCA continued to handle the academy's federal funds until 1990, when the LSC became its primary fiscal agent, a change that is still in place.

The academy's federal funding has itself come in diverse forms. Perhaps the most significant of these is the federal money the program received as a "Basic Skills Improvement program" from 1980 to 1982, which allowed for great expansion. This expansion—as well as the changes discussed in previous paragraphs—shows how the academy's funding sources have influenced its affiliation and function.

State and federal funding for the programs has been supplemented by donations from individuals, local organizations and businesses, and programs like the United Way. LARA also supplements support by holding fundraisers, such as the annual LARA Spelling Bee that Jaclyn and Allen participated in (but didn't win). Figure 2.4, which is adapted from the 2007–2008 "How LARA is Funded" handout distributed with the "Volunteer Training Manual," illustrates this complex financial relationship.

A major change to the academy occurred in 1998, when the federal Workplace Investment Act was passed. Title II of this act, Adult Education and Family Literacy, changed adult education nationally by requiring federally funded adult education programs like LARA to include workplace preparation. Again, these broader national changes shifted LARA's identity, including its relationship with other programs in the area and even its name.

LARA's website explains that the new funding required the organization to partner with the Workforce Investment Board and also that programs would be required to "meet performance objectives in areas of skills improvement, employment, secondary accreditation, and post-secondary education." In 2001, the academy changed its name from the Lafayette Adult *Reading*

How LARA is Funded

Final Figures for 2007 - 2008

State Dollars	Federal Dollars
$547,111	$387,663

Indiana State Department of Education
↓
Local Education Association - Lafayette School Corporation
↓
United Way
Business & Industry
(Kiwanis International, Lilly, Dollar General, Wabash National, Wal-Mart, etc.)
Commuity Organizations
↓
Lafayette Adult Resource Academy
(Financial and Non-Financial Donations)

- State and Federal Cost per Registered Learner: $529.02
- State and Federal Cost per Enrolled Learner: $549.54
- State and Federal Cost per Contact Hour: $ 7.61

Figure 2.4   How LARA Is Funded

Academy to the Lafayette Adult *Resource* Academy to reflect its expanded curriculum.

Like its funding structure, LARA maintains a complex organization. The table in figure 2.5 details the instructors and others working under the director, who is responsible for supervising and interacting with all teaching and administrative staff, as well as the advisory board. As reflected in the 2007–2008 LARA annual report, the state of Indiana organizes LARA into the categories illustrated in figure 2.5.

Function	Adult Education Personnel		Unpaid Volunteer
	Part-time	Full-time	
State-level Adminstrative/Supervisory/Ancillary Services	0	0	0
Local-level Adminstrative/Supervisory/Ancillary Services	19	2	931
Local Teachers	10	0	71
Local Counselors	1	0	65
Local Paraprofessionals	11	0	260

Figure 2.5 Adult Education Personnel by Function and Job Status

The LARA annual report (2007–2008) notes that "the number of unpaid volunteers assisting with ancillary services reflects the large number of community individuals who either helped with fund-raising or contributed financially to LARA."

LARA Needs

During early meetings with Suzanne and visits to the program, the authors learned about LARA's need to establish objectives and demonstrate gains. In that first visit, for example, Allen and Jaclyn observed numerous students and teachers holding yellow documents that resembled file folders. Suzanne identified these documents as the "Instructional Learner Record" (ILR) and explained that they were used to articulate objectives and track student progress. Suzanne explained that before students leave LARA each day, teachers mark their progress or time studied on the document.

The ubiquity of the ILR to LARA's day-to-day work is important for several reasons. For one, the document contains space to articulate specific objectives from a list of possibilities like passing the GED or gaining employment. To the authors, Suzanne wearily explained that carefully articulating objectives is crucial to LARA's work, as the program's funding relies on percentage of objectives met in a given year.

More specifically, instructors must avoid marking too many objectives, since the ratio of objectives met to objectives articulated matters. At the same time, instructors are motivated to mark objectives, since they cannot count a gain a student makes if that gain was not originally noted on the ILR. For example, if a student gets a job while studying at LARA, the program cannot count that positive change in their annual report if the student did not mark "gain employment" as an objective when he or she began study, even if the student gained employment as a direct result of LARA instruction.

As Jaclyn and Allen observed use of the ILR and listened to Suzanne's explanation, they considered their own experiences in the writing center. These experiences helped the authors understand the pedagogical function of the ILR, as well as LARA's larger need to identify student-learning goals, assess learning, and document outcomes. Though LARA and the Writing Lab differ in many areas, use of regular documentation and assessment offers one common characteristic that allowed the university and community partners to understand each other's work.

For example, a visitor to Purdue's Writing Lab would probably wonder about the pre- and post-tutorial forms used during tutoring sessions, as LARA visitors would wonder about the ILR. Like the ILR at LARA, the Writing Lab's forms serve a pedagogical function and allow students and tutors to negotiate goals and track progress. They also allow tutors to communicate with one another and, sometimes, the students' instructors. At LARA and the Writing Lab, such forms recognize that students will learn from multiple people who benefit from being able to quickly review the students' goals and previous work.

Additionally, LARA's and the Writing Lab's forms serve administrative functions. As she was learning about the ILR, Jaclyn thought about her courses in writing program and writing center administration, where she learned about how documentation supports funding by tracking usage and gains and ultimately showing that programs are worthy investments.[4] However, it became clear in early meetings and observations that LARA's funding model necessitated documentation that was far more painstaking than anything the authors had witnessed in the university context.

Another key difference between the Writing Lab and LARA concerns their attention to students' personal lives. The Writing Lab and LARA share an outreach mission, but the Writing Lab's scope is purely academic and occasionally professional. On the other hand, many LARA projects acknowledge different areas of community members' lives, including work, family, education, and life skills.

This attention is crucial to LARA's mission of outreach to the community, a mission that seeks to not only draw people into the program's doors but also to impact their lives on several levels. This work includes the Outreach Family Literacy project, GED classes at the satellite branch at the Tippecanoe County Jail, and workplace training projects for employees at many of the community's largest employers. All of these examples illustrate one of LARA's main missions—to meet students, sometimes literally, where they are, and to help them improve their lives.

In recent years, key partnerships have allowed LARA to further expand. In particular, LARA has developed its attention to workplace preparation and the local economy. A key change was establishing a WorkOne Express site in the same building as LARA. The proximity of the WorkOne (Indiana's state employment agency) site to LARA allows for smoother connections between education and employment.

LARA has also collaborated with the Lafayette Urban Enterprise Association (LUEA) and Tecumseh Area Partnership (TAP). LARA's partnerships with WorkOne, LUEA, and TAP demonstrate the program's interest in collaboration and its dedication to economic and community development. These commitments provide further evidence of why LARA was a great partner in university-community engagement.

The WorkOne Express Center

As noted above, LARA and WorkOne Express have been partners in community literacy and employment for well over a decade. This partnership began in 2001–2002 when WorkOne Express co-located with LARA at the Ross Loeb Building in downtown Lafayette. This partnership continued when LARA and WorkOne Express moved to the old Washington School on Elizabeth Street (LARA website). But the origins of WorkOne date back to the 1930s and Roosevelt's New Deal, as Allen learned from an early email and subsequent interviews with the WorkOne site coordinator, Sam.

In response to the crippling effects of the Great Depression, Roosevelt and a sympathetic Congress created a number of relief, recovery, and reform initiatives. These initiatives included the Department of Workforce Development and the Wagner-Peyser Act of 1933 and established the groundwork of federal and state supported programs that helped train people who were unemployed and connect them with employers seeking skilled, educated workers (Wagner-Peyser Act Information Web page).

To streamline these efforts during the Clinton administration, Congress amended Wagner-Peyser with the Workforce Investment Act in 1998. One of the goals of this act was to establish a coherent career pathway where employers could connect with skilled workers through one-stop delivery systems, like LARA/WorkOne Express. During visits to LARA and WorkOne, as well as during conversations with the community partners, the authors heard regularly about the programs' goal of being a one-stop system.

The WorkOne center is located at the end of a main hall in the old Washington School, where job training posters and fliers for Alcoholics Anonymous meetings dot the walls. A WorkOne visitor walking down the hall will see, in what was once the school's cafeteria, piles of donated interview suits on old lunch tables. A quick glance inside the cafeteria reveals people looking through these suits while they gather for a job interview workshop. Many are minorities or single parents with children who play quietly around them.

Entering the WorkOne computer lab, once a science classroom, a visitor will notice the sign-in desk and computers humming away on long tables pushed up against the walls. A large bookshelf leans against a long table where people sit and skim through the *Journal and Courier*, Lafayette's local newspaper. A visitor might also see WorkOne clients pecking away at the computers; some clients are obviously disheartened by their search for employment. One person sighs audibly as she tries to complete a job application for McDonald's. Her daughter draws pictures on a wrinkled piece of paper that lists her mom's job history, which ends some time ago.

While the center sometimes bustles with activity and other times sits empty, this downcast scene represents an average late morning during an average week at WorkOne. One of the stark differences Allen and Jaclyn noticed when moving from the world of higher education at Purdue, then adult education at LARA, and finally employment assistance at WorkOne is the somberness of the WorkOne center.

While the college campus crackled with youthful optimism, and LARA bustled with conversation and second chances, WorkOne felt markedly *older* and more serious. The people at WorkOne, in some cases, were there because they *had* to be there on work release from jail or because they were under- or unemployed. Most WorkOne clients were experiencing hardship that seriously impacted them and their families, and that hardship affected the center's mood and feeling. As someone who has experienced adult education and underemployment first hand, Allen felt acutely aware of this shift in mood from optimism, to second chance, to last chance.

The WorkOne Express center that shares a building with LARA is part of the statewide employment agency that Indiana maintains through a network of regions. Lafayette is located in Region 4, which includes Tippecanoe County and eleven other counties in northwest Indiana. WorkOne's main goals include providing statewide job information, as well as offering employment training and assistance.

WorkOne accomplishes these goals in cooperation with the Indiana Department of Workforce Development. In addition, WorkOne partners with the nonprofit, JobWorks, Inc., to train and assist people searching for employment. Lastly, WorkOne assists people in filing for unemployment through the IN.gov website and provides access to federal and state government employment opportunities (WorkOne Indiana website).

Face-to-face services at WorkOne include basic employment workshops and workshops on writing cover letters and résumés. To facilitate these workshops, the center maintains its computer lab stocked with twelve machines that have Internet access. The computers also run employment assistance software to help users choose and prepare for a career path. Computer programs include Mavis Beacon Teaches Typing, ACT's KeyTrain and WorkKeys, WinWay Resume Deluxe, and Rosetta Stone.

To aid in the job search process, the center also has a phone, a printer, and a copy/fax machine. Volunteers maintain a small library filled with books on jobs, cover letters, résumés, employment applications, taxes, housing, finances, and family issues. Some of these resources are in Spanish. Other resources include work clothes (the suits in the cafeteria), eyeglasses, bicycles for transportation to jobs, and bus tokens to get to WorkOne; these resources are nonfinancial gifts from local businesses (LARA/WorkOne Yearly Report).

WorkOne's total operating budget for 2008–2009, the time period the authors collected this data, was $56,877. The center is supported not only by the state but also by a complex network of public and private concerns in greater-Lafayette. These organizations include foundations established by for-profit companies to assist the community. Nonprofit support comes from organizations like Lafayette Community Development, LUEA and TAP (see previous section), United Way, and the Fairfield Township Trustees.

The center maintains one part-time employee, Sam the site coordinator, who works with LARA volunteers to staff the lab from 8:30 a.m. to 5:00 p.m. Monday through Friday. The coordinator and volunteers assist with computer instruction and job search writing needs. LARA volunteers also help WorkOne users fill out online job applications, file for unemployment benefits, and write cover letters and résumés. A LARA volunteer also helps Sam record use-and-outcomes data for the LARA/WorkOne yearly report.

The people who use WorkOne Express, as mentioned above, represent the general population of greater Lafayette, excluding faculty and students affiliated with Purdue. WorkOne users represent local residents seeking assistance with employment and/or filing for state unemployment benefits. According to Sam, some WorkOne users have completed GED, ESL, or high-school programs at LARA, are seeking jobs in greater Lafayette or other parts of the state, and come from working-class backgrounds.

The total number of WorkOne users in 2007 was 6,007, but in 2008, that number jumped to 8,745, no doubt due to the recession. The number of new visitors also increased: In 2007, WorkOne enrolled 915 new users, while in 2008, 1,148 new users visited the center (LARA/WorkOne Yearly Report). Due to the recession that began in 2007, some WorkOne users had been laid off from jobs at local industries, such as Wabash National, Tate and Lyle, Alcoa, Caterpillar, Subaru of Indiana Automotive, and other smaller businesses.

WorkOne clients who entered the workforce remained low. Though LARA and WorkOne operate well-organized programs, the unfortunate truth is that larger economic forces usually determine the employment futures of those who visit the center. In 2007, only 1.98 percent of WorkOne users reported successfully entering the workforce. In 2008, that percentage was 2.38. While this percentage represents a slight increase, it demonstrates how difficult it was to obtain employment in greater-Lafayette at that time. Unemployment hovered around 13 percent during the collaboration with LARA/WorkOne (LARA/WorkOne yearly report).

WRITING THE ENGAGEMENT PROJECT

Up to this point, this chapter has focused on the less formal process of getting to know the community partners and beginning the project. Formalizing the partnership and project involved writing for a variety of purposes and audiences. This writing included the capstone project proposal for the public rhetorics course, which evolved into proposals that the authors submitted to the Writing Lab and to LARA/WorkOne. Other documents included the extensive IRB application forms with attendant material, four grant proposals (three of which were funded) and ultimately, prospectuses for Jaclyn and Allen's separate dissertations.

Often, writing scholars omit the types of writing they must complete to engage in community-based work, an omission the authors hope to address here. This book seeks to illustrate the full process of civic engagement, including positives and negatives. Toward that end, shared next in this chapter are the messy processes of writing to propose, outline, fund, and complete the CWEST.

In many ways, the CWEST came to life as the authors wrote for it in its early stages; essentially, Allen and Jaclyn wrote the project into existence as they were meeting with colleagues and potential community partners. These colleagues and community partners, therefore, became co-authors who shared key institutional history and cooperation, as well as information about needs and expectations.

The capstone project for the graduate public rhetorics course was a project proposal that the authors composed after meeting with the community partners and reading relevant scholarship. This, however, was not to be a simple project proposal; the document had to be augmented with scholarship and a detailed bibliography, which would demonstrate that Jaclyn and Allen were well informed about a risky area of engaged scholarship, the type of scholarship where academics leave the hallowed halls and venture off campus and possibly get into trouble.

More specifically, engaged scholarship (discussed in detail in chapter 6) is high stakes because missteps can mean damaged community relations. If the authors wanted to pursue this project, they had to prove their ability, their well-developed plans, and their caution to professors and the Writing Lab staff. They also had to earn the trust of the community partners and prove their sincerity, two measures that had at least begun through the meetings discussed above.

The capstone proposal ended up at thirty-three single-spaced pages; graphics and tables, as well as headings, added to the page count. The proposal included, among other elements, an introduction with timeline and budget overviews; a background with information on the stakeholders and an overview of relevant theory; possible research methods; a proposal of the actual work to be done; and appendices with literature reviews.

When Linda Bergmann saw this behemoth proposal, she smiled and said, "This is great, but you're going to need a shorter proposal for your community partner." Linda already knew what Allen and Jaclyn had learned from meeting with LARA administrators: they would not have the time to read such an extensive document. The revised proposal excluded information the community partner already knew, such as their organization's background, and academic information, such as the literature review. The proposal did not outline research methods and questions: developing those would come later, and in collaboration with the community partners.

The proposal for LARA and WorkOne ended up being seven single-spaced pages. All stakeholders signed this proposal as an indication of understanding and commitment. Once the proposals were completed, it was easier to imagine the timeline for the CWEST. To help contextualize the project, the authors present an overview of that timeline and stages of the CWEST here, though later chapters explain this timeline in more detail.

The timelines included in the original proposals were very ambitious. Jaclyn and Allen originally thought that the CWEST could be completed by 2008, but the project ended up taking two years longer than anticipated. These delays were first caused by complications with Purdue's IRB (see next section). In retrospect, the authors realize that such an ambitious project had to be completed in the longer timeline they ended up following. Each stage described below included numerous meetings with LARA/WorkOne teachers and staff.

Stage 1, CWEST Development, spring 2007 to spring 2008: produce literature review, project proposals, IRB forms, and grant proposals; begin developing GED resources and collecting data; post GED resources.

Stage 2, ESL Material, summer 2008 to spring 2009: develop and post ESL resources; conduct usability tests on both GED and ESL resources; revise resources and CWEST area on Purdue OWL.

Stage 3, WorkOne Material, spring 2009 to spring 2010: develop and post WorkOne material; conduct usability tests and revise WorkOne resources; conduct quasi-experiment with pre- and post-test cover letters and résumés from WorkOne end users.

Despite their feelings of accomplishment having met with LARA/ WorkOne staff and completing the proposals, Allen and Jaclyn's elation was short lived as they composed the end-of-term presentation for the public rhetorics course. As they completed the presentation to be given on the final exam day, the authors realized that the project was going to take a long time to complete. Moreover, it began sinking in that even though the proposals seemed organized, the project itself was likely to be messy and might fail. At this point, the stakes were pretty high as the authors nervously presented the work to their peers and began seeking IRB approval.

RESEARCH METHODS AND SEEKING IRB APPROVAL

Chapter 3 presents the research methods in more detail, but this section provides a general overview so that readers can better understand the IRB process discussed later in the section. From the outset, the authors decided they would use a mixed-methods approach to research the project. As noted in chapter 1, Simmons and Grabill's (2007) piece, "Toward a Civic Rhetoric for Technologically and Scientifically Complex Places" strongly influenced this and other decisions about the research methods.

Unique to Simmons and Grabill is their focus on collaborative knowledge building between researchers and participants, thereby shifting the epistemological center from the ivory tower into a shared, generative space. They argue that this type of rhetorically informed empirical approach is imperative if scholars are to work effectively with community partners: "Such a rhetoric . . . must concern itself with understanding how people create civic cultures, how they define themselves within recognizable public spheres . . . such a rhetoric, in other words, must be empirical" (p. 439).

The methods Simmons and Grabill (2007) suggest include helping communities empower themselves through epistemological means. They state that citizens "must be able to produce the professional and technical performances expected in contemporary civic forums . . . meeting notes and agendas, flyers and newsletters, websites and iMovies, meetings and protests, letters and reports" (p. 422). While Jaclyn and Allen would draft the literacy resources they thought they might develop with LARA and WorkOne, the community partners would be involved in the composition and testing process as much as possible to share in the knowledge building.

In early stages of the research, before any materials had been developed, the authors hoped to learn as much as they could about LARA, including its student and teacher population, the learning environment, the teachers' pedagogies, and the program's administrative characteristics. Qualitative methods, including focus groups, observations, and interviews, allowed for gathering the type of contextual, nuanced information that the authors sought about the program, its learners, and its teachers.

In later stages, the authors used qualitative and quantitative methods to obtain data on materials. These stages of the research were recursive, meaning that Allen and Jaclyn moved back and forth among developing, researching, revising, and posting all three areas of resources (GED, ESL, and workplace writing literacy). In addition to interviews and open-ended survey questions, they used rating scales, Likert scales, time-on-task, mouse click, and navigation path methods. Many of the research methods used at these later stages were borrowed from technical communication research.

Aside from informal conversations during early meetings with LARA and WorkOne administrators, all of the research described in the preceding paragraphs required IRB approval. To the authors, the task seemed daunting initially, even with the help of their mentor, Linda Bergmann, and a fellow PhD student, Dana Driscoll. Two main issues made the IRB process particularly overwhelming:

1. The project was iteratively designed and combined civic engagement and empirical research, two points that seemed to confuse the Purdue IRB.
2. The project involved at-risk participants, LARA/WorkOne users who had been traditionally marginalized; most participants were low income, many were minority and/or Spanish speaking, and some had dropped out of high school or had been incarcerated.

Despite these challenges, the authors stumbled through as best they could, and what follows explains the process and overviews the IRB documents.

One of the unique and valuable features of the project design was that the authors collected data from various participants at different points in the design process. This approach is known as iterative design, which basically means that researcher-developers collaborate closely with users to compose and then test deliverables in multiple stages. Further, the authors collected both qualitative and quantitative data, which provided different kinds of insights about the project.

One of the early pioneers of the iterative approach is Pelle Ehn. Ehn (1992) influenced the CWEST project because he wrote extensively about the value of designers and users interacting in participatory, democratic ways. This approach mirrored the authors' collaboration with LARA/WorkOne. Because democratic approaches are important for developing mutually beneficial college-community relationships (see Cushman, 1996, 1999), the authors followed Ehn's (1992) recommendations of including stakeholders from the beginning of the project.

As the following quote suggests, Ehn (1992) emphasizes stakeholder participation for both philosophical and practical reasons. Ehn writes that participatory design can work toward more democratic collaborations and can also yield better products:

> Participatory design raises questions of democracy, power, and control at the Workplace . . . the other major feature is technical—its promise that the participation of skilled users in the design process can contribute importantly to successful design and high-quality products. (p. 1)

While a participatory approach is optimal for collaborative projects, it confused Purdue's IRB office. For example, the IRB insisted that the authors provide all details, protocols, questions, and informed consent forms for the entire three-year study up front. Though the IRB office assured the authors that amendments were possible, when Jaclyn and Allen tried to explain to them that data from early stages of the project might suggest the need for changes to the process, protocols, or questions, they balked.

Moreover, the combination of community-based work and empirical research seemed foreign to Purdue's IRB. IRB reviews were divided into different disciplinary categories based at the university, and the social sciences reviewers were confused by a community-based research project. Reviewers repeatedly asked the authors if the project was service-learning or research. Also, Allen and Jaclyn were challenged about how they would conduct usability testing, even though their methods followed best practices in professional writing. For example, reviewers asked how the authors could guarantee participant anonymity if the test materials were online.

Jaclyn and Allen soon realized that part of what they were doing was educating their IRB in a process that combined elements of teaching, research, and engagement. The IRB proposal created a number of hurdles to clear, not the least of which was the traditional concept of civic engagement that the university fostered. The university understood the categories of extension, outreach, and service-learning, but the Purdue IRB offered no boxes to check for a project that combined teaching, service, and research. Apparently, the university had never completed a community-based research project like the one the authors were proposing.

Completing the IRB proposal required making some new boxes on the forms, metaphorically. This triggered numerous emails from confused administrators and IRB reviewers, but the authors addressed these challenges by corresponding with the IRB through email and phone calls over several months and by completing what seemed like endless revisions of their forms. By the time the authors actually met with the IRB representatives, it was December of 2007, seven months after the original proposals had been submitted to the Writing Lab and LARA/WorkOne.

The authors were behind schedule and nervous. December holiday breaks, when many IRB staff members went on vacation, complicated the initial meeting with the IRB and the IRB renewals for years to come. The delay in IRB approval meant that Jaclyn and Allen could only meet with the community participants and not collect any real data. Before the project had even gotten off the ground, the authors were experiencing some of the messiness of community-based work.

Once the IRB office understood the project, they required an extensive amount of documentation, which included a letter of approval from the community partner, samples of participant recruitment fliers, protocols, and interview questions. This delayed the process even more as the authors had to ask an administrator from LARA to write a letter and wait for its completion.

During this time, another challenge arose: since some of the participants were Spanish speakers, the IRB stated that the authors would need to provide recruitment fliers and informed consent forms in Spanish. These documents had to be created by a trained Spanish translator in the modern languages and literatures department and approved by their translation supervisor. In one final exasperating delay, all of the IRB forms had to be switched from first-person to third-person perspective "due to a recent policy change."

In the end, the IRB agreed to approve the first set of documents for Stages 1 and 2, the GED and ESL resources, and to then review Stage 3, WorkOne, at a later date. The Stages 1 and 2 IRB packet clocked in at six pages of forms and thirty pages of attendant material. The authors discuss the IRB process here not to complain or characterize the procedure as trivial or unnecessary. The need to protect participants and to follow standard procedures is critical to university-community partnerships. Rather, this information is shared to further a practical discussion about conducting community-based research.

FUNDING THE PROJECT

In the initial project proposal, the authors considered it a point of pride to say that the project could be completed at almost no cost to stakeholders. Allen and Jaclyn thought, incorrectly, that stakeholders might be more inclined to collaborate if it would not cost them much to do so. Linda Bergmann pointed out that while university partners had to be cautious about how much money they requested and spent, they also should not send the wrong message about the quality and worthiness of projects.

Linda would often say, "If you tell your institution that you can work with little or no support, people will take advantage of your hard work. Or, when budgets get tight, they will cut your funding altogether, thinking that you'll do the work for free." After the project proposals were approved, Linda suggested reviewing all of the potential expenditures to develop a detailed budget. She was preparing the authors for the next stage of the CWEST project: requesting support.

After refining the research methods and the project timeline, Jaclyn and Allen were able to think through possible costs related to the CWEST. While wrestling with the IRB office, they developed a budget and anticipated the following expenditures for stage one (all estimates):

- Participant reimbursement: LARA teachers and learners—$15 each: $600
- Interview transcription: ~20 hours at $10/hr.: $200
- Miscellaneous costs (gas, food, flier copies, recording equipment): $200
- Subtotal: $1,000

After meeting with LARA administrators and teachers and reviewing their computer capabilities, the authors learned that they needed at least one new computer to run one part of the GED resources Jaclyn was developing, the GED Essay Game discussed in chapter 3. LARA's older PCs could access all of the other online literacy resources, but LARA teachers thought that a GED game might be useful. The authors added the request for a new computer that would run Adobe Flash to the stage one budget, which brought the total to $2,000.

For stage two, the authors estimated a similar budget, minus the new computer, because WorkOne had new machines. The budget totaled $1,000 and was based on the following estimated expenditures:

- Participant reimbursement: WorkOne volunteers (two) and WorkOne users—$15 each: $600
- Interview transcripts: ~20 hours at $10/hr.: $200
- Miscellaneous costs (gas, food, flier copies): $200

The total request from supporting stakeholders was $3,000. The authors had a number of options for granting organizations, including Purdue groups and outside institutions. Funding opportunities within Purdue fell into three categories that reflected the university's long-standing mission of teaching, research, and service: teaching with technology, research, and community outreach. The next type of writing, then, involved writing proposals for these opportunities.

To meet the readers' needs, the authors tailored each proposal to the purpose of each grant, and they were successful in gaining the funding. The authors stopped looking for support after learning that Purdue would fund the CWEST. Pursuing external support would have been useful, but other parts of the project had to take priority. Specifically, the authors had to prioritize completing the IRB process, developing the literacy resources with LARA/ WorkOne, and beginning to collect data.

The kind of writing described in this section—writing to get the projects started, to build relationships with stakeholders, to get approval for research, and to obtain funding—is easy to overlook but central to developing and sustaining community-based work. The next chapter switches focus from this kind of "behind-the-scenes" work to the "star" of the CWEST project: collaborating with LARA and WorkOne to develop adult educational resources for the Purdue OWL.

As discussed in the preface, this book supports the claim that writing centers can form effective spaces for university-community collaboration with two areas of information about the CWEST: the empirical and iterative process that guided it, and the personal relationships that held the work together. Chapters 1 and 2 have focused on the personal relationships and the empirical-iterative process used, as well as some of the theories that helped inform the CWEST. Chapter 3 details the process used to develop the first set of literacy resources, the GED material; the chapter also presents the initial findings from this stage of data collection.

NOTES

1. Suzanne later acted as a research participant, so her name has been changed to protect confidentiality. All research participant names are changed throughout the book.

2. The GED test is currently in a state of change. The authors refer here to the form of the exam in place when the project was being developed. See the epilogue for discussion of how changes to the GED exam suggest the need for ongoing community engagement in this and other adult education projects.

3. Since its inception, LARA has operated under three different names: (1) the YWCA Reading Academy (1976–1979), (2) the Lafayette Adult Reading Academy (1979–2001), and (3) the Lafayette Adult Resource Academy (2001–present). These name changes are significant to LARA's identity, mission, and role in the community. To simplify, the authors refer to LARA as the "Academy" or LARA throughout the book.

4. For more discussion of the connection between engagement and administration, please see Jaclyn's essay, "Writing Program Administration and Community Engagement: A Bibliographic Essay," published in Rose and Weiser's (2010) *Going Public: What Writing Programs Learn from Engagement.*

Chapter 3

Methods and Findings from Stage One
Developing the GED Resources

This chapter picks up the story after IRB approval and financial support were secured and Allen and Jaclyn were beginning to collaborate with LARA on the project's major deliverable: the CWEST, a section of the Purdue OWL with resources tailored to adult students. This chapter covers the next three steps in the model from chapter 1, with the addition of one step: Present, Publish on Project to Get Feedback (see figure 3.1). This additional step illustrates the authors' evolving and ongoing efforts to share the project in scholarly venues.

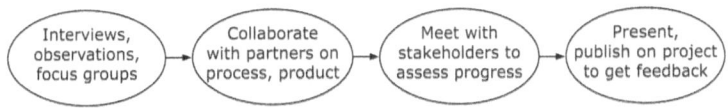

Figure 3.1 Detailed Research and Assessment Steps

Among the three major areas targeted for the CWEST—preparation for the GED exam, ESL, and workplace and job search literacy—GED resources were most lacking. Though the OWL's existing ESL and workplace resources were not tailored to the adult students' level, the OWL offered *no* resources about the GED or any other standardized exam.[1] All partners decided, then, to draft GED materials first. Production of ESL resources followed, and last came the workplace and job search materials.

Jaclyn took the lead on developing the GED resources, as she had the most experience with basic writing instruction. Tony Cimasko, a graduate student with ESL expertise, helped develop the ESL resources. Allen took primary responsibility for the workplace and job search resources, as he had the most experience teaching professional writing. Though Jaclyn, Tony, and Allen divvied up the work, they collaborated throughout the process.

Development of all CWEST resources included recursive processes of researching, drafting, revising, and posting materials to the OWL. While the timeline generally followed GED first, ESL second, and workplace resources third, this process overall was far from linear or neat: The authors went back and forth among the groups of materials and moved regularly among drafting, revising, researching, and posting the materials. For the sake of clarity, this chapter and the next follow the general timeline in their descriptions of resource development.

The first half of this chapter describes the development of the GED resources. In many ways, the process of developing, revising, and posting these materials to the OWL was more challenging than the process of doing the same for the ESL or workplace materials. The GED resources were first, and creating resources for a standardized exam presented unique challenges. The authors begin by describing the GED resources, then, not only because they were the first group of materials developed, but also because their development illustrates the full range of challenges faced throughout the project.

A PICTURE OF A COMMUNITY EDUCATION PROGRAM: INITIAL RESEARCH FINDINGS

To develop materials that would work for LARA and WorkOne students and teachers, Jaclyn and Allen needed to learn about their missions and goals (see previous chapter), as well as their day-to-day workings. The authors knew from their own teaching experiences how basic characteristics of the teaching context affect practice. In one example, the limited printing allowance in Purdue's English Department greatly affected instructors' day-to-day course planning.

In a more positive example, instructors like Allen and Jaclyn enjoyed regular access to computer lab time, as all of Purdue's first-year composition sections met in the computer lab weekly, and professional and technical writing courses did so entirely. Even observers with general knowledge about teaching college writing would not fully understand the day-to-day classroom practice in Purdue's writing courses without knowing about the program's context, including access to resources like printing and technology. The authors knew the same would be true of LARA and WorkOne.

The first part of Jaclyn's research used interviews and observations of four teachers to investigate LARA's teaching context. This research provides an example of how findings were applied to practice throughout the project.

By interviewing instructors and observing their teaching, Jaclyn was able to provide important information about LARA's day-to-day practices and challenges, including teaching strategies, available resources, and constraints.

The teachers Jaclyn observed and interviewed were candid about their experiences and perspectives, partly because the collaboration had been going on for several months at this point. As they had worked with the Purdue OWL in the past, they were also able to offer feedback about how the OWL currently did and did not meet their needs. The information collected during this phase of the research allowed for more effective GED resources and later, more successful ESL and workplace resources. The information also helped the authors think about the CWEST's design on the OWL.

Jaclyn's most valuable research findings[2] shed light on how teaching in the adult education context differs from teaching at the university level. From the beginning of the project, the authors acknowledged that LARA and WorkOne differed greatly from the university teaching context. Jaclyn's findings pushed this further and challenged some the authors' buried beliefs that they had more in common with LARA and WorkOne teachers than they did not. Jaclyn's research findings made clear that the differences in context created more differences in teaching practices than the authors could have imagined.

Interestingly, the authors often found the most in common with LARA teachers when drawing on their experiences in the writing center. Pedagogically, LARA teachers spoke often of asking students regularly about *their* needs, which reminded the authors of the customary agenda setting in writing center sessions. Administratively, LARA teachers talked about documenting their work to protect funding, a strategy that reminded the authors of Linda Bergmann's advice to "count everything" in the writing center.

LARA's space provides helpful clues about the program's workings. Most teaching at LARA happens in the building's main "learning lab," a large room sectioned off by the placement of desks, bookshelves, and tables. The main section of the room looks most like a traditional classroom, with twenty-five or so individual desks facing a large chalkboard. In the corner sit several computers in a group, and in another corner are a cluster of shelves with various textbooks. Along the far wall are larger tables for group tutoring sessions.

Like Purdue Writing Lab staff and staff in university writing centers all over the country, LARA teachers have divided their larger space into smaller areas to meet the program's needs. In the Writing Lab, the space mainly accommodates one-on-one tutoring sessions that are the hallmark of writing center work, while at LARA, the space is deliberately set up to support a variety of teaching configurations, including classroom-based, small group and pair sessions, and individual study.

From observations and interviews, Jaclyn learned more about support for diverse teaching and learning styles at LARA. During an interview, one teacher, Ann, responded simply, "whatever works, works" when asked to describe her teaching strategies. She explained that after twenty-five years of teaching in the adult education context, she had come to view herself as a maître d' of sorts. Ann's job, she believed, was to keep track of all the different methods and resources available for learning, help figure out with students what works best for them, and "serve up" the curriculum accordingly.

All of the teachers talked about individualized instruction, and observations supported their remarks. During one typical observation, Jaclyn watched two teachers split the twenty or so students in the learning lab into two groups. During a one-hour observation, one teacher, Joan, asked one student to write a paragraph on the computer and then offered holistic feedback on it; drilled another student out loud on multiplication tables; and sat side by side to help a student work through a practice GED exam. Even by the standards of writing center pedagogy, this level of flexibility was impressive.

Jaclyn's findings about LARA's available resources shaped the CWEST the most. During interviews, the teachers described the program's limited budget for study materials and explained that many of their textbooks were outdated or in bad shape. They described supplementing published textbooks with handouts, many of which had been developed by LARA teachers over the years.

The program did have several computers, some of which were equipped with software for studying for the pre-GED and GED exams. This software was not free—LARA had to pay for it, just as they did for GED textbooks. Additionally, the software was not online but was loaded onto those computers, so students and teachers could not access the programs to study for the pre-GED and GED at home or in libraries.

Also relevant was the degree to which students and teachers gravitated toward online and computerized resources. Generally, research suggested that online and computer-based resources for the GED were limited, but the authors were cautious about assuming that teachers and students *wanted* such resources. Perhaps not surprisingly, the findings in this area were mixed: Some teachers and students did want options for online and digital resources, while others did not seem bothered by the lack.

LARA teachers generally respected student preference about working on the computer. Some teachers, however, did limit student Internet use. One particularly vocal teacher explained that if students were looking at inappropriate sites, her own reputation was at stake because she had to log onto the machines to get to the Internet. School records, then, would have her identifying information logged as the "user" who pulled up the inappropriate material. Further, LARA's jail branch, where weekly GED prep courses were offered, maintained computers but did not provide access to the Internet.

Lack of Internet offers one example of how Allen and Jaclyn tailored the resources to meet the programs' needs. All of the resources were converted to downloadable PDFs so that teachers could access and run copies of handouts they used often. Additionally, all of the resources were saved to CDs. LARA was given several copies of the CDs so that teachers could access the materials on the computer without going online, if they preferred.

Having the resources as downloadable PDFs would also, the authors hoped, make the resources more attractive to those who preferred print resources and add to the body of print handouts the teachers had collected over the years. The binders of these handouts were reminiscent of what Jaclyn and Allen had seen in writing centers and composition programs over the years. From their experience as teachers and tutors, the authors recognized those binders and did not want to let the OWL's status as a major online resource overshadow the importance of having effective print handouts at the ready.

Research findings also showed that LARA and WorkOne students themselves had limited resources, especially in comparison with Purdue students. Within reason, the authors could ask students to purchase whatever texts and supplies seemed necessary for their writing courses. Additionally, they could assume that most students owned their own computers and had home access to the Internet, and many students owned other useful technologies like digital cameras, video and photo-editing software, and e-readers.

Further, the university could generally provide much of what students did not have. Student computer labs at Purdue were many; laptops and cameras could be rented from the IT department; and campus buildings were equipped with free wireless Internet. In contrast, students at LARA and WorkOne were typically from the low-income group and had fewer resources; the teachers explained that few students could purchase study materials like GED prep textbooks and that many did not have computers or Internet at home. LARA was less able to provide what students did not have (particularly not for home use).

These last two points left the authors in a conundrum. Like the rest of the OWL, the CWEST resources would be free, of course; this would help students who did not have the means to buy textbooks. On the other hand, the materials would be online, so students without computers and Internet would not be able to access them from home. This chapter, and future chapters, includes fuller discussion of how this and other issues were handled, but in general, research participant and LARA teacher, Ann, provided an answer to this particular conundrum.

When Jaclyn wondered whether all of the students would be able to access the CWEST, Ann responded cheerfully, "Nope." When the authors hesitated, puzzled by her enthusiasm, Ann reiterated the need for many materials to accommodate various needs and preferences. "My role," Ann said, "is to figure out what the student needs and wants in here and point them to it. Some students like online stuff and can get online at home."

Ann continued by saying that on the other hand,

> Some of our students don't have the Internet at home, and others have the Internet but still want print resources. I need a bunch of different resources to point people to, and you guys are adding to what's available. That's always a good thing, even if not everyone winds up using what you make.

Ann also noted that CWEST materials would at least provide a free online *possibility* for self-study, even if not all students would be able to access the resources at home.

DRAFTING THE GED MATERIALS

The GED materials differed from other Purdue OWL resources in one major way: they were designed specifically to help students pass an exam. Despite potential philosophical problems with standardized exams, teachers at LARA, like in other adult literacy organizations elsewhere, are committed to helping students achieve the goals they set for themselves; reaching high-school equivalency is among the most common reasons why students come to LARA and similar programs.

CWEST materials, then, needed to support successful completion of the exam. The difference between this goal and the goal of other OWL resources should not be overlooked. While the GED resources could help students gain knowledge about writing and language for general, professional, and academic use, the materials needed to also impart knowledge about how to take the test. This was particularly true of the resources on the timed writing portion, as writing an essay in forty-five minutes would present new challenges for many test takers.

To create effective materials, then, Jaclyn needed to learn about the exam itself, rather than just the *content* it tested. This included information about the exam's structure, focus, and scoring. Jaclyn began developing the GED resources by looking at print GED preparation books. LARA had many of these onsite, and the Writing Lab purchased a couple of the books to help support the CWEST development. The books looked similar to preparation books for other standardized exams, and quickly took Jaclyn back to days prepping for the ACT and GRE.

The writing part[3] of the GED exam contained two elements: a multiple-choice section and an essay. The seventy-five-minute multiple-choice section included fifty questions about four areas: organization, sentence structure, usage, and mechanics. The forty-five-minute essay presented a topic of common knowledge and typically asked writers to state and explain their opinion. Two independent graders scored essays on a four-point scale based on four areas: main points, organization, development of ideas, and sentence-level correctness.

Two key goals emerged as Jaclyn drafted the resources. First, she wanted to avoid overwhelming test takers. During interviews, all the instructors discussed their students' past and present challenges in school; a constant challenge, they noted, was keeping students from becoming overwhelmed or discouraged. The GED exam could seem particularly daunting, as testing anxieties added to the pressure.

Second, Jaclyn wanted to follow the format and content of the exam as closely as possible. Based on instructor comments, the authors imagined that most students would not look at multiple resources—such as CWEST material *and* a published book—in preparation for the exam. Jaclyn felt pressure, then, to make sure the materials did not mislead test takers with incorrect or confusing information about the format or content of the GED.

The first drafts of GED preparation materials followed the format of the exam. Just like the exam, the resources were in two groups: a group for the multiple-choice section of the writing exam and a group for the essay. To explain the test itself, Jaclyn included three handouts: one that explained the writing exam overall, one that specifically explained the multiple-choice section, and one that explained the essay, including its scoring.

Materials for the multiple-choice section covered the four areas tested by that part of the exam: organization, sentence structure, usage, and mechanics. Within each set of materials were sample questions that resembled what test takers would see on the GED. Materials for the essay section followed the four areas scorers look for when assessing: main points, organization, development of ideas, and sentence-level correctness.

Essay materials included example essay topics, as well as sample thesis statements, outlines, and paragraphs. While looking through all of the material drafts, Jaclyn noted places that could link on other sections of the existing OWL when the materials went live. The authors and LARA instructors hoped that this would provide direction to students who wanted further study without overwhelming those who were exclusively focused on GED preparation.

FIRST REACTIONS TO THE GED RESOURCES: A FOCUS GROUP

Initial feedback to the GED resources occurred in a focus group with the four LARA instructors who participated in Jaclyn's research. This focus group informed the first major revision of the GED section of the CWEST, before Jaclyn's second-round interviews and observations gathered additional feedback. The focus group in many ways paralleled the first meeting with LARA's assistant director. In both the cases, Allen and Jaclyn's level of enthusiasm for the work was so high that disappointment was inevitable.

That enthusiasm was particularly high given the polished product the authors had to present (printouts organized painstakingly in a binder with sheet protectors, a clear reflection of their shared and abundant love for office supplies). In truth, these first drafts largely reflected the authors' own teaching preferences: The binder of materials even resembled Jaclyn's own collections of teaching resources. The first go at developing CWEST materials shows that Allen and Jaclyn were still learning how to collaborate with teachers whose experiences, pedagogies, and teaching contexts differed from their own.

The one-hour focus group met at one of the large tables in LARA's learning lab. The conversation was audio recorded. Each of the four participants received print copies of all of the drafted materials. Initially, the participants expressed enthusiasm and gratitude for the resources. As the discussion continued, however, many of the materials' shortcomings came to light.

The focus group format allowed for a highly productive—if slightly deflating—experience because the participants could riff on one another's suggestions. Within this discussion, they offered many comments about their teaching experiences at LARA, so the authors obtained information about their pedagogy that added to the findings from the first round of Jaclyn's interviews and observations. The discussion also provided a complex understanding of how the teaching materials would (and would not) fit into instruction at LARA.

The instructors offered three major criticisms of the materials. First, the resources were not sufficiently interactive; all four instructors wanted to see more exercises and activities. Second, the materials were written at a comprehension level that was too complicated for LARA clients; the instructors suggested that the authors use Microsoft Word's readability check (the Flesch-Kincaid measures) to help adjust the reading level. Finally, the materials contained too many long passages of text that might intimidate or overwhelm students.

This third point about the long passages of text is important for thinking about the recursive (even messy) process of developing and revising resources while designing the online space that would house them. More specifically, Jaclyn and Allen could not separate development and revision of the materials from decisions about how to present them on the OWL. As the authors asked for ideas about how to break the text into smaller sections, they thought constantly about what those sections might look like online.

The instructors reiterated many of the same claims about their pedagogy, experiences, and teaching context that they had made during Jaclyn's first round of interviews. A general theme came to light repeatedly during the focus group: The lovely, polished binder of materials may have been perfectly useful for a traditional teaching context and students, but students came to LARA specifically because the traditional environment had not worked for them. The long blocks of text, lengthy explanations, and black-and-white pages would do very little besides intimidate LARA's students.

AFTER THE FOCUS GROUP: INITIAL REVISIONS TO THE GED RESOURCES

During the focus group, the authors learned that they had not thought carefully enough about LARA's student population and how it differed from Purdue's. Despite following Simmons and Grabill's (2007) suggestions and Ehn's (1992) participatory approach, they still had not created resources that fully matched the partners' needs and expectations. With the focus group's findings in mind, Jaclyn began revising the GED materials, and both authors began thinking about how to present the finished products on the OWL.

The revision plan seemed fairly straightforward: break up longer sections of text; decrease the reading level with shorter, clearer paragraphs, sentences, and words; and develop more interactive exercises. When actually revising the GED materials, Jaclyn was challenged to consider a different population of students than she was accustomed to teaching. Similarly, when thinking about how to design the CWEST section of the OWL, Allen and OWL webmaster Jeffrey Bacha were challenged to consider a different population of users (see fuller discussion of this topic later in the chapter).

Jaclyn began by breaking resources into smaller sections, thinking as she did about potential OWL organization strategies to suggest to Allen and Jeffrey (see fuller discussion of taxonomies later in the chapter). Throughout the project, the authors learned that they could not separate the materials' pedagogical effectiveness from their usability; this realization was perhaps never clearer than during this phase of the project, when Allen and Jaclyn were taking on their first major revision while they and Jeffrey were thinking through how to present materials on the OWL.

In addition to breaking resources into smaller sections, Jaclyn improved the readability of the materials by shortening sentences and paragraphs, clarifying language, and incorporating more bulleted lists and headings. Jaclyn and Allen had learned to make similar revisions with their own teaching materials, like handouts and assignment sheets, since students are likely to skim such documents.

With the GED resources, the need for clear language, short sentences and paragraphs, bulleted lists, and headings became even greater than in the authors' own teaching materials, because the CWEST would be posted online, where users are perhaps even more likely to skim. Additionally, as the instructors pointed out during the focus group, the students at LARA had generally lower reading levels than the students Jaclyn and Allen taught in courses at Purdue.

The final revision, developing more interactive resources, presented the greatest challenge. The authors could make the materials more interactive but were limited by time, resources, and technical expertise. The Purdue OWL itself presented constraints. For Jaclyn and Allen, it was unrealistic to create highly interactive games or flashy graphics, as the OWL could not support them.

However, it was possible to include more of the exercises that the instructors had praised during the focus group. These "exercises" were really just practice questions of the kind that students would encounter on the multiple-choice section of the writing exam. Though basic, these exercises added a useful dimension to the GED preparation materials because they allowed users to get practice with the content and format of the exam.

Revising the GED essay resources for greater interactivity proved far more challenging for Jaclyn than developing more exercises for the multiple-choice portion of the exam. Multiple-choice questions are simple to develop and post online. But, how does one create an interactive experience for practicing a timed essay? Fortunately, Jaclyn was taking a course—her last in the PhD program—that helped solve the problem.

The course, Samantha Blackmon's New Media Studio, was designed to include equal parts theory and production. Rather than expect students to be experts at new media production or formulate perfect final products, Blackmon encouraged even novices like Jaclyn to consider the rhetorical nature of composing in unfamiliar software applications. It was settled: Jaclyn needed a course project, and the GED essay resources needed greater interactivity. With that, the GED Essay Game was born.

Jaclyn created the game in Adobe Flash. The process felt intimidating, as she had no knowledge of Flash and little knowledge of Photoshop, which she also needed for editing images. Blackmon and fellow PhD student Mark Pepper helped Jaclyn learn Flash well enough to produce the game. Without flashy animation or music, the final product looked less like a "game" than readers may be imagining. Despite its limitations, though, the game achieved what earlier GED essay resources had not: It was interactive. See figures 3.2 and 3.3.

The game focused on process and guided students through a procedure of timed writing with GED essay-like questions. LARA instructors had lamented during interviews that many students skipped the planning stages when faced with the GED essay, a tendency that could lead to poorly

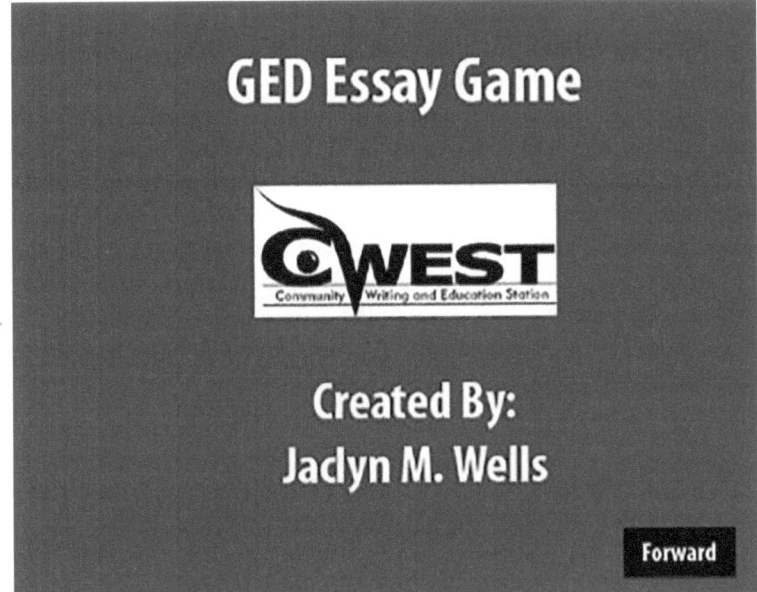

Figure 3.2   GED Essay Game, Slide 1

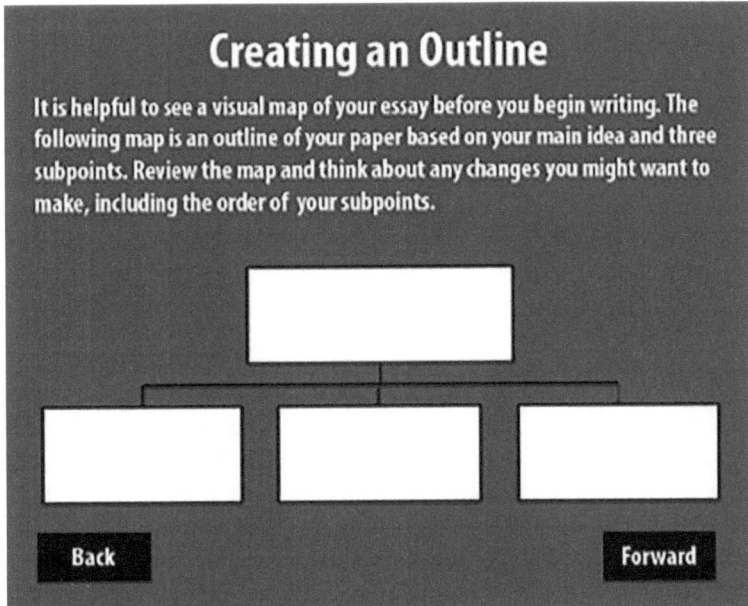

Figure 3.3   GED Essay Game, Slide 2

organized or incoherent writing. In the GED Essay Game, users were given an example essay prompt and then taken through the full process of prewriting, drafting, revising, and editing an essay.

The prewriting stages included heuristics to brainstorm ideas, draft a thesis, and make an outline. Users typed all of their responses in the game itself, and Jaclyn created buttons so that they could move back and forward among different parts of the process. During research interviews, LARA instructors had also mentioned that students struggled to complete the entire writing process in the exam's limited time. The game instructions advised users to time[4] themselves while going through the different steps, so that they could practice condensing their whole writing process down into the forty-five minutes allotted by the exam.

INSTRUCTOR RESPONSE TO THE GED RESOURCES: ROUND TWO INTERVIEWS AND OBSERVATIONS

After the GED resources were revised, they were published on the Purdue OWL. Like all the CWEST resources, the GED section would be revised numerous times after this initial publication. Jaclyn's round two interviews and observations provided insight for the next major set of revisions. These interviews and observations focused on investigating how LARA instructors used and responded to the GED preparation resources after they were posted to the Purdue OWL.

Jaclyn's findings suggested that most importantly, LARA needed a variety of resources to support individualized pedagogy; this finding suggested that CWEST resources were useful inasmuch as they provided another option—and a free online option, at that—for instructors to use with students. In addition to this general finding, the authors learned that LARA instructors needed particular kinds of resources. The sections below describe some of the program's most important resource needs and explain how these needs relate to the CWEST.

The Need for Flexible Resources

During interviews, the research participants suggested that they would continue to rely primarily on published print GED preparation resources, but they also indicated that the CWEST materials provided an additional option. Alice, the LARA instructor who worked at both LARA and the jail, explained that having the materials available would support the individualized instructional methods that she and other LARA instructors already use.

Alice's comments below represent claims made by all four of the teachers during interviews:

> Since we already run a pretty individualized program, I just see this [CWEST resources] as having one more resource to have available to the learner for whom it is going to be the most appropriate fit. I don't think it is going to change the way that I do work but I do think it is going to give me a good resource for a subject area that I have really been struggling to find good materials for.

Importantly, Alice emphasizes finding resources that are "the most appropriate fit" for the learner. In many cases, the most appropriate resource for a student might not be an online resource like the CWEST, which is something Jaclyn and Allen had to accept throughout the project. Alice's comments reminded the authors of Ann's advice early in the project, when she cheerfully stated that some students wouldn't use the CWEST at all but that the resources provided one more option.

During three of the four observations, CWEST GED materials were not the primary resources in use. The exception was Jaclyn's observation at LARA's jail branch, where a greater percentage of students used CWEST materials than during the three observations at LARA's main learning lab. At the jail, the instructor, Alice, helped a small class of a dozen inmates prepare for the GED. This class met weekly, and Alice explained to the authors that she had led it for years.

Surprisingly, GED study at the jail more closely resembled a traditional class than what the authors had observed in LARA's learning lab. The session involved a lecture and discussion with the whole group, followed by individualized writing and other exercises that some students did on the computer and others did by hand. This balance of lecture, discussion, and individual work resembled what Allen and Jaclyn both did regularly in their own courses. Additionally, most of the students were young; many of them were close in age to the authors' students at Purdue.

During the GED class, Alice accessed the CWEST materials on the CDs the authors burned for all of the instructors (as noted previously, the jail branch has computers but no Internet access); upon her request, the authors had provided extra CDs for use in the GED classes at the jail. Alice explained after the observation and during her interview that many of the students at the jail branch preferred working on the computer, so the CWEST materials had proven particularly useful in that context. The next section includes more discussion of LARA's need for both digital versus print materials.

Digital and Print Resources

As discussed earlier in the chapter, the authors only distributed print drafts of the materials to the instructors to facilitate the focus group. When they learned during the focus group that the teachers actually *wanted* print versions of the resources, Jaclyn and Allen grew concerned about how valuable they would find the CWEST at all. If they preferred print handouts to online, would the CWEST resources really be that exciting?

After the resources were published on the Purdue OWL, instructors did indeed continue to primarily use published GED resources because many of their students preferred print materials. However, during the interviews, instructors clarified that having the digital CWEST materials would help support the program's commitment to respecting student learning preferences. And some students, they explained, did enjoy or even prefer using materials on the computer.

Alice, for example, explained what Jaclyn had observed in the GED classes at the jail, that many of these students enjoyed exercises that they could do on the computer. She witnessed this preference in LARA's main learning lab as well: "A lot of my guys, and I think it is true here [the learning lab] too, they love working on the computer, so getting to do an exercise . . . that is computerized is more fun."

Alice's comments again reminded the authors of their own students. In first-year composition courses, Allen and Jaclyn often witnessed with amusement how the same students who quit writing after just a couple of minutes when asked to write with pen and paper would write multiple paragraphs when asked to write on the computer. This provides one example of how the authors' teaching experiences would sometimes parallel those of LARA teachers. While the teaching contexts differed greatly, the authors could benefit greatly from staying attuned to those moments when the experiences did overlap.

Finally, the instructors discussed the challenges of managing the environment of the learning lab. In the lab, instructors are resources that must preserve their time and ration it fairly among the many learners present. Using Internet resources can complicate this. Specifically, instructors noted that waiting for resources to load could take a long time; using digital resources would require instructors to provide extra assistance to students who are unfamiliar with computers; and using Internet resources would require teachers to monitor students to make sure they were staying on track.

Because LARA instructors have so little time with each student, these extra time commitments can be challenging. The instructors' comments reminded the authors of how much usability mattered, particularly since many LARA students are less comfortable than traditional students with Internet resources. This again supports the idea that the authors could not separate revising the content of the resources from revising how they appeared on the OWL: the two were inseparable.

Guided and Independent Instructional Resources

Instructors also indicated that they needed resources that facilitate guided instruction and independent learning. They explained that some students who attend LARA require guidance from instructors, whereas others prefer to work almost entirely on their own. Alice discussed using the CWEST in both guided instruction and independent learning in her GED preparation classes at the jail. Like the class that Jaclyn observed, most jail classes include a mix of whole-class or group lecture, activities, and/or discussion followed by hands-on individual work.

In addition to use in the jail classroom or the learning lab, Elaine and Joan commented that the resources would be useful for self-study outside of LARA. Elaine commented that students "will be happy to know that they can find something like this so that they can do practice at home." Though they did not say so directly, Elaine and Joan may have considered the CWEST good for independent learning because it is freely available for everyone's use, whereas LARA's other resources are available only onsite. In earlier interviews, they emphasized that students could not take any resources home.

Observations supported interview findings that LARA instructors used the CWEST for both independent learning and guided instruction. However, the observations also showed that for some LARA learners, using the resources independently required the instructor to first teach some basic computer skills. Generally, guiding LARA students to CWEST resources required more than simply giving the student a URL.

Observations of Ann and Elaine at the main LARA location illustrate this finding very clearly. Ann worked with Terry, a GED student who was preparing for the multiple-choice portion of the writing exam. After opening the CWEST site and showing Terry the different resources, Ann directed her to the verb tense materials, including a couple of exercises. She briefly showed her how to use the resources before leaving Terry to work on her own.

During Elaine's observation, Jaclyn witnessed a nearly identical situation, as Elaine spent nearly ten minutes introducing a student, Trey, to the CWEST resources before leaving him time to work independently. In both Elaine's and Ann's observations, the students used CWEST materials successfully and independently, but only after the materials had been introduced and explained thoroughly. This finding supports instructors' concerns about the amount of time that CWEST materials could require.

Joan's observation even more clearly demonstrated the role of instructors in students' successful use of the CWEST. Joan worked with Natasha, who, like Terry and Trey, was studying for the multiple-choice section of the GED writing test. Joan directed Natasha to the apostrophe materials and introduced her to an exercise to practice inserting apostrophes.

After Joan left, Natasha became frustrated when she was unsure of where the apostrophe button was located on the keyboard. She initially confused it with the comma button and became even more frustrated when she realized her mistake but did not know how to use the backspace button. When Joan came to check on Natasha's work, she showed her the apostrophe and backspace keys. Though Natasha was then able to complete the exercises, it was clear that she was frustrated.

While observing at the jail, Jaclyn saw the mix of guided instruction and independent learning that Alice described in her interview. Alice began the class with a sentence-combining activity that the students did together. She distributed a handout with an explanation of sentence combining and a number of choppy sentences. As a class, Alice and the students worked through the handout, discussing different ways to combine the sentences. CWEST resources were not used during this portion of the class, but were used during the next half, when students worked independently on the GED essay.

Alice opened the GED Essay Game for the three students who wanted to work on a computer. She asked Jaclyn to show the students how to use the game (more on this experience in chapter 5). After a quick tutorial from Jaclyn, the students were able to work independently using the GED Essay Game until the class ended. It was clear, again, from this observation that independent study of the CWEST resources required computer assistance from the instructor. Interestingly, the game actually seemed to require less explanation than the other less interactive CWEST resources.

Transferable Resources

LARA's limited funding means that the program cannot afford many resources, so the resources that they do have are more valuable when they can be used for many different students and situations. Instructors commented that the CWEST may be useful for students studying for similar standardized tests or for students who simply need help with writing.

For example, Elaine suggested that GED preparation materials may be useful for students preparing for the Compass test, an exam with a similar format to the GED that many local community colleges use to help place students into appropriate courses. She commented that her students "have passed the Compass 100% when we have used the GED materials" and that the CWEST "would be very helpful to people wanting to pass the Compass test too because the format is the same."

Despite these comments, all of the students who used the CWEST materials during Jaclyn's observations were studying for the GED. The one exception was Terry, who Ann explained was actually a pre-GED student based on her testing. Terry got through the CWEST GED exercises with difficulty, suggesting that LARA's existing pre-GED resources might have been more appropriate for her. Ann noted this after the observation.

Terry's case illustrates that even though some LARA instructors may transfer resources, those resources must match the learner's level. Comparing the interview findings with the observation findings suggests that the CWEST GED preparation materials were actually more appropriate for a non-GED student (like those studying for the Compass test) than for pre-GED, even when those pre-GED students have the eventual goal of taking the GED. When it comes to transferring resources, what matters most is the students' learning level.

Interactive, Level-Appropriate Resources

Even after revisions following the focus group, the interview findings suggested that the resources could be even more interactive and overall level appropriate. When asked to comment on the GED resources, Elaine responded that the materials still required the students to do a lot of reading: "There is still a lot of reading. And a lot of folks are not inclined to do a lot of reading. Or they get lost because to them it is boring. Or it is just too much information."

Elaine pointed out that many LARA learners have attention and reading comprehension problems that make unwieldy and long resources even more problematic: "They are the same people who don't do too well on the reading test because yeah, they understood everything they read when they were reading it but that was in that paragraph but in this paragraph it is like, 'What did I read up there?' Minds wander."

The other three participants also made it clear that they preferred the interactive materials to other CWEST GED resources. All four instructors noted that they had used or would use the multiple-choice exercises and GED Essay Game with students, even if they had not or did not prioritize using the other materials. This reinforced what Jaclyn saw during observations, when nearly all of the students who used GED resources used the exercises or the game.

Joan noted that some of her ESL students enjoyed using the game and exercises, even though they were not studying for the GED; this relates to the earlier point about the necessity for transferable resources. Ann pointed out that the choice of whether to use the game depended upon the learner's preference: "There are people that like games and it is motivating for them and then there are other people that don't want to do them." Her comments reinforce that instructors choose materials based on the learner's preferences and learning styles.

Revisable Resources

Finally, interview findings suggest that LARA needed resources that were updated to change with the continual changes in adult education. In particular, the instructors commented regularly that the GED itself changes frequently. This finding has significant implications for the CWEST's future, which the authors discuss in more detail in chapter 6 and the epilogue.

Broader changes in adult education may also influence the CWEST's use and necessary revisions. Ann discussed these changes toward the end of her interview, when Jaclyn asked if she had any other comments on the CWEST. Ann emphasized the possibility of funding cuts, which she claimed could make the CWEST materials more important for LARA and other adult education organizations.

Specifically, Ann said,

> The fact that you have a product that can be easily used by other people without a whole lot of teacher interaction is extremely useful because the funding for adult education is getting worse and worse . . . we are almost in survival mode. We haven't had any increase in funding for over 10 years.

Ann's remarks imply that funding cuts may create a greater need for free instructional resources that adult students can use independently. Though Ann commented that the CWEST can be "easily used by other people," some findings (discussed above) suggest that teacher interaction was necessary to guide students to the materials and show students how to use them.

Based on these findings and Ann's point that independent study may become more common in the future, the authors knew that they needed to revise CWEST materials so that they were easier for students to use independently. Making the resources easier to use during independent study meant thinking about the resources' usability on the Purdue OWL. The next chapter focuses on how the materials were posted online and made usable for adult education teachers and students.

NOTES

1. The OWL did contain resources (about writing process, mechanics, grammar, etc.) that could help students learn the content tested by the GED exam. As discussed later in this chapter, though, understanding the format of the exam itself and practicing test-taking skills are important to preparing for the GED and other standardized exams. Prior to the CWEST, the OWL did not contain any information about test taking, and few free GED resources were available online.

2. For a fuller discussion of Jaclyn's (spring 2014) research findings, please see her article, "Investigating Adult Literacy Programs through Community Engagement Research: A Case Study," published in the *Community Literacy Journal*.

3. The community partners briefly discussed also including preparation materials for the reading section of the GED. Ultimately, the authors decided that given their limited resources, time, and expertise, it would be best to focus entirely on the writing section. Additionally, LARA teachers emphasized during interviews and informal conversations that they were more in need of study resources for the writing section of the exam, especially the essay.

4. These instructions illustrate the limitations of resources designed by graduate students with limited experience in new media production. Ideally, the game itself may have included a timer (though pedagogically, one could make an argument that self-timing creates less pressure). Jaclyn did not learn this particular feature of Adobe Flash, as it was lower on the list of priorities than more basic parts of the program.

Chapter 4

Methods and Findings from Stages Two and Three

Developing the ESL and Job Document Resources

As chapter 3 makes clear, drafting the GED materials was only a first step. Once drafting was complete, Jaclyn began the first of many revisions and Allen began working with the Purdue OWL Webmasters, Dana Driscoll first and Jeffrey Bacha later, to organize the CWEST area in the OWL's new Engagement section. The previous chapter should also make clear that drafting and revising CWEST resources was closely connected to the process of developing this new OWL section. The authors could not think about breaking up the resources into manageable parts, for example, without thinking about how those parts would look online.

Though these processes of drafting and revising resources and designing the OWL are inseparable, this chapter focuses primarily on the design of the Engagement section and the development of the next set of resources. This chapter begins by describing the OWL design process, including the usability testing the authors employed, and concludes by explaining Allen's work with WorkOne on job search documents. This chapter also covers development of ESL resources. As such, the chapter explains the next step from the model and highlights the value of the iterative process the authors followed, as illustrated in figure 4.1.

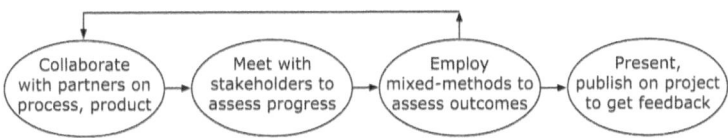

Figure 4.1 Mixed-Methods and the Iterative Process

REVISING THE RESOURCES AND POSTING THEM TO THE PURDUE OWL

While Jaclyn began the formal research for the CWEST—observations, interviews, and focus groups—Allen contributed to some of the questions asked regarding the organization and design of the CWEST section of the OWL. These inquiries included LARA teachers' preferences for organization and page layout. These inquiries also included obtaining information about technology use at LARA, the complexity of which surprised the authors as they continued developing online and print CWEST materials for their diverse population of users.

Fortunately, Allen and Jaclyn were not starting the work from scratch. The LARA teachers had used the Purdue OWL before, and so they were familiar with its setup. Moreover, Allen had worked on the Purdue OWL usability project begun in 2006,[1] so he was familiar with the OWL's strengths and limitations, as well as the research methods the authors used to tailor the CWEST resources to the community partners' needs.

Technology Use at LARA

From the outset of the collaboration with LARA, it was clear that the teachers and staff needed sustainable literacy resources that could be accessed at multiple points within the LARA building, as well as external locations like the public library and county jail. The resources also had to match LARA clients' diverse learning needs and styles. Moreover, LARA teachers and staff stated that the resources had to be updateable to keep up with changing pedagogical requirements.

These needs necessitated placing CWEST resources on the Purdue OWL. Housing the resources in this online space came with a couple of additional advantages. First, since some LARA teachers, staff, and volunteers had used the OWL, the new CWEST resources would not be in a totally unfamiliar environment. Second, the authors and community partners agreed that CWEST resources could prove valuable to other adult education teachers and students. Housing the materials on the OWL would allow the partners to share these new resources with users worldwide, and the OWL's reputation could possibly help these resources become widely used.

Though the advantages of putting CWEST resources on the OWL were clear, the authors also learned that technology use at LARA ranged widely and created some concern. LARA clients included users who were comfortable in digital environments and users who were, as one participant put it, "technologically nervous." Some users, LARA clients who were either highschool dropouts or recent immigrants, did not even have keyboard or mouse training, and so were mostly unfamiliar with the Internet or using graphic-user interface to navigate pages and websites.

Generally, the authors discovered that technology use among LARA clients fell into the following categories:

- Recent immigrants and older adults: little or no technology experience
- Younger adults and high-school dropouts: moderate technology experience but mainly with applications like search engines, social media, and email

Technology use among LARA teachers, staff, and volunteers was also important. The authors discovered that technology use among this population fell into the following categories:

- Older teachers, staff, and volunteers: little or no technology experience
- Younger teachers, staff, and volunteers: moderate technology experience but mainly with applications like search engines, social media, and email. One exception to this was experience with databases, which a small number of LARA staff maintained because they used a database to run and analyze data for the annual report and grant proposals

To address these usability and design issues, Allen worked closely with Dana Driscoll, the OWL Webmaster at the time, to organize an Engagement section of the OWL that could be dedicated to community engagement projects. Writing Lab Director Linda Bergmann strongly believed that a separate Engagement section would help organize the OWL's rapidly expanding resources and draw attention to the writing center's community engagement work. Usability concerns for the CWEST area of the OWL fell into six categories. Below, these are listed in descending order according to importance based on findings from the OWL usability project.

Regarding the CWEST, Jaclyn and Allen asked:

1. Will users feel comfortable navigating resources?
2. Will users know where the resources they need are located?
3. Will users know how to access the resources they need?
4. Will users successfully find and use the resources they need?
5. How long will it take users to access the resources they need?
6. How many mouse clicks will it take for users to access the resources they need?

Organization and Design Challenges

Having just worked on the Purdue OWL usability project,[1] Allen realized that the organization of the CWEST area would present one of its major challenges. The Purdue OWL contains many writing resources, and even a semiautonomous area within the OWL can easily get confusing when not organized effectively. Based on OWL usability project findings and on scholarship and best practices in Web design, the authors knew that the CWEST would have to be organized in general to specific categories and then individual pages. This approach was also the most effective way of addressing the six questions outlined above.

To achieve these goals, Allen and Jaclyn planned on composing two overall sections—LARA and WorkOne. Within these sections, they planned to include subsections, such as GED lessons and ESL lessons. Moreover, the authors believed that they would need a third level of taxonomy (organization scheme) that would include separate categories for individual pages. These individual pages would be about different areas of the GED exam, for example.

A major roadblock to this design was the lack of a three-tiered taxonomy for the entire OWL. When Dana Driscoll, the OWL Webmaster, graduated, the new webmaster, Jeffrey Bacha, assumed responsibility for the in-house content management system. The difficult task of reprogramming the Purdue OWL now fell upon Jeff, but the three-tiered taxonomy could not be launched until after the first round of CWEST testing was completed. The authors suspected that the CWEST, and perhaps even the entire OWL, needed a three-tiered taxonomy. But a decision this important required empirical research; this process is discussed a little later in the chapter.

Designing the CWEST pages was also challenging. Most importantly, the authors knew from the initial feedback explained in chapter 3 that the pages would need to be clear and easy to use. The pages couldn't be text heavy or difficult to read. In fact, after the focus group sessions, the LARA assistant director asked that CWEST content maintain a Flesch-Kincaid readability score of 7.0–8.0 and a Flesch reading ease score of 60–70.

Allen and Jaclyn used these readability measures to help compose content even though many scholars in professional and technical writing have resisted such approaches (see Duffy, 1985; Redish and Seltzer, 1985; Schriver, 1993; Connaster, 1999; and Mazur, 2000). Essentially, the authors tried to keep the CWEST content at an 8th grade reading level because the community partner wanted it that way, and respecting the partner's expertise and wishes was paramount. Once the GED resources were revised and posted, the next step was to collaborate with ESL instructors at LARA to compose the second language material.

Developing the CWEST ESL Resources

The second type of resources LARA teachers asked for were materials for second language, or ESL, students. These resources included grammar and mechanics lessons, such as content on punctuation, pronouns, and sentence combining. Like other resources the authors were developing with LARA and WorkOne, the OWL had plenty of materials on these areas, including material geared for ESL work; however, these resources were not tailored to the needs and learning levels of LARA's adult students. This was why it was so important to collaborate with a graduate student ESL specialist in the English department, Tony Cimasko.

Tony and Allen used interviews and observations with LARA's ESL specialist to learn about needs before drafting ESL materials. Interview and observation findings suggested that LARA clients needed the most help with paraphrasing, prepositions, pronouns, sentence combining, punctuation, and discourse connectors (therefore, however, etc.). With these areas as his focus, Tony got to work on the resources.

Once Tony had drafted the ESL resources, he and Allen met again with the ESL specialist for feedback. Based on this assessment, Tony revised the resources, and Allen posted them to the Purdue OWL. At this point, both GED and ESL resources were housed in the new Engagement section of the OWL and the entire section was ready for the first generation of usability testing. These tests followed a mixed-methods approach.

GENERATION ONE TESTING

Allen has published elsewhere on both generations of CWEST usability testing.[1] Rather than detailing this process here, then, the following sections overview the methods surrounding this stage of the project.

Research Methods

As noted above, research methods for this stage of the CWEST project were informed by the Purdue OWL usability project (Brizee, Sousa, and Driscoll, 2012), as well as scholarship from professional writing (Coe, 1996; Sullivan and Porter, 1998; Dumas and Redish, 1999; Nielson, 2005; Theofanos and Redish, 2005). Of particular interest were the mixed-methods models these scholars suggest and outline in detail. Specific data collection consisted of demographic surveys, as well as qualitative and quantitative measures using the following procedures (many test resources are included in the appendix).

The qualitative data included three areas: interviews, open-ended questions on questionnaires, and artifacts. Interviews ran iteratively as the authors learned about LARA teachers' and learners' needs and expectations, developed resources, and collected feedback to improve those resources. The open-ended questions were included on the after-test questionnaire in the usability tests. Finally, the authors collected LARA artifacts such as

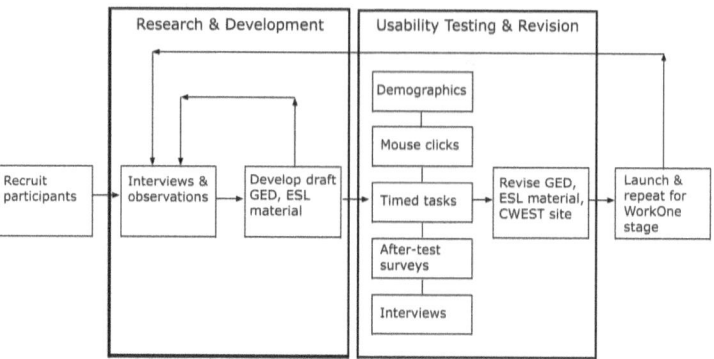

Figure 4.2   CWEST Generation 1 Testing

marketing materials, fliers, and budget reports, some of which have been discussed in previous chapters.

The quantitative data included two areas: usability tests and after-test quantitative surveys following them. The usability tests used three methods: (1) time-on-task was tracked to measure how long it took participants to find information on the CWEST; (2) mouse clicks were counted to measure how many link selections participants used to find information; and (3) navigation paths were recorded to analyze participants' surfing and decision-making tendencies. Following the tests, participants filled out questionnaires with Likert-scale questions that sought to gather their impressions of the CWEST site and resources.

The flowchart, figure 4.2, illustrates the Generation One testing process.

Once Jaclyn had revised the GED resources, and once Tony and Allen had collaborated with LARA specialists to develop and post the ESL materials to the Purdue OWL, the CWEST was ready for testing. Tests took place at LARA in a small office containing one desktop computer, and participants were tested one at a time. Participants filled out a demographic survey, completed four tasks asking them to find information on the CWEST, filled out an after-test survey, and then completed an interview. Jaclyn and Dana recorded mouse click, time-on-task, and navigation path data while Allen proctored.

Participants

To recruit participants, Jaclyn and Allen emailed and spoke with LARA administrators and teachers. Unfortunately, the authors were not able to recruit as many end-user participants as they would have liked, LARA clients, but they were able to work with a few. Participants were reimbursed $10 for their time. For the first generation of testing, where the authors analyzed the GED and ESL resources, the thirteen total participants included both LARA staff and clients.

The majority of participants for the first generation of testing were LARA administrators, teachers, and/or volunteers. All nine of these participants were females. These participants had diverse backgrounds and experiences, as well as mixed training. The administrators and teachers had graduate degrees or were certified teachers, whereas volunteers were retired teachers or community activists.

Participants also included four LARA clients (three females, one male). LARA clients had not completed high school or earned GEDs. The three female clients came from families comprised of immigrant agricultural or service-industry workers, while the one male participant came from a family with a manufacturing background. All four LARA learners were minorities with mixed English-speaking skills from challenging socioeconomic situations. Two of the female learners were single parents and came from backgrounds of addiction and incarceration.

Data Analysis

Informed by Dumas and Redish (1999) and Anselm Strauss (1987), Allen used descriptive statistics and grounded theory to analyze and triangulate data. Allen also used descriptive statistical analysis for the GED and ESL usability testing and calculated means, medians, frequencies, scores, and variability of scores. Specifically, he used descriptive statistics to analyze and triangulate time to complete task-based protocols, number of mouse clicks to complete protocols, and means of Likert-scale ratings in the after-test questionnaire from the usability tests.

To provide a user-centered and participatory method of analyzing the qualitative data, Allen used grounded theory to analyze data from interviews and open-ended survey questions. Allen read the qualitative data and identified where participants discussed ideas related to the research questions and then developed theories that matched the dataset. Specifically, Allen followed micro- to macro-level analysis (Driscoll, 2009) by using the participant responses to build categories. From these categories, he developed participants' ideas of terms like "usable" and "sustainable."

Generation One Test Findings

Overall, participants responded positively to the project itself, and they found the GED and ESL resources to be fairly usable. The authors conclude this based on participant concepts of terms like "helpful" and "usable" gleaned from the process of grounded theory analysis. Rather than imposing their ideas of key concepts, Allen and Jaclyn tried to measure the success of the CWEST and the usability of its resources based on participants' ideas of these assessment terms. Put another way, the authors operationalized assessment terms based on participants' definitions.

Qualitative data: Interested in both process and product, the authors asked participants in generation one of the testing what they thought about the CWEST project and the Writing Lab-LARA collaboration overall. One of the participants, Diane, responded:

> Oh, I think it [the LARA-Writing Lab relationship] is really important. I think it is a good mix. . . . That's gonna' make it just more user friendly with the learners. . . . I am gonna' be more inclined to take them to this website now that I have actually had a session.

Like Diane, most people who worked with the authors during the first set of tests were optimistic about this project, even when they were hesitant about the ongoing relationship between the Writing Lab and LARA. The final part of Diane's response provided a surprising and valuable bit of information: Jaclyn and Allen had not realized the training and awareness-raising potential of usability testing when beginning the project.

The authors also received valuable suggestions from participants; these are a good example of the participatory approach sought throughout the CWEST project. Once again, participants suggested simplifying the content. Audrey, a LARA teacher, stated:

> So I'm wondering if it needs [to be] more clear. If people are needing help, ESL people or GED people, they won't read this much and they probably won't comprehend what they've read.

In addition, participants wanted a print option for the online resources, and they wanted to move the search box from the upper right side of the pages to just above the navigation bar on the left side of the page. Other participants did not even see the search box and also suggested moving it. One LARA teacher requested a CWEST "how-to" resource. Lastly, many participants suggested adding a site map, a resource OWL staff had wanted for some time. This final point illustrates how this community-based project resulted in unanticipated benefits for the Writing Lab and OWL, as the authors were able to gather data on the OWL from nonuniversity users.

Quantitative data: Usability findings were positive overall but indicated some problems. For the first generation of tests on the GED and ESL resources, participants took on average 187.87 seconds to complete the three tasks (the fourth task was speak aloud, so the authors did not collect data on mouse clicks or time to complete task).[2] It simply took users longer than what is ideal to find materials.

Additionally, participants used on average 2.33 mouse clicks to complete the tasks. This was not a negative amount given the authors' goal of 3–5 clicks, but participants only completed 60 percent of the tasks (the 3–5 mouse-click goal was based on findings from the Purdue OWL usability project [Driscoll, Salvo, Brizee, and Sousa, 2008]). Although these quantitative scores seemed positive, overall results indicated problems with usability. The post-test surveys and interviews verified these problems and provided additional support that a mixed-methods approach best allows researchers to see the full picture of online resources' usability.

For post-test feedback beyond the interviews, the authors collected data on a five-point Likert-scale survey where the lower score indicated participants' unsatisfactory impressions with the website and writing resources. While survey results showed that participants did not find the website and resources unusable, the scores indicated that Jaclyn and Allen could do more to fulfill the participants' needs. On a 1–5 scale, participant total average impression scored a 3.05, or high neutral—not great considering how much time and effort had gone into the iterative design process to this point.

Revisions Based on Research Findings

Based on the quantitative and qualitative findings from the first round of testing, the authors followed all of the suggestions above. However, the site map, print button, and "how-to" page could not be added until after the second generation test. The resources' word count was also reduced. To make navigating and using the website and resources easier, the authors reorganized the site taxonomy and navigation bar from a two-level to a three-tiered design. Figure 4.3 shows the original GED/ESL site, and figure 4.4 shows the GED/ESL site after revisions.

Though the navigation bar in figure 4.4 is full, only the pages available in Part 1 Lessons 1–4 are visible. The GED Practice pages are embedded behind the second-level link, "GED Practice." To make the search box more visible, the authors moved it from the upper right side of pages to the top of the navigation bar on the left.

Allen and Jaclyn had both looked forward to receiving feedback from the community partners to see how the work was faring. However, after the mixed responses received on the literacy resources and the CWEST site, the authors did some serious rethinking of the project. While they were pleased with some of the outcomes, the material and the online environment that housed it were not as usable as the authors would have liked.

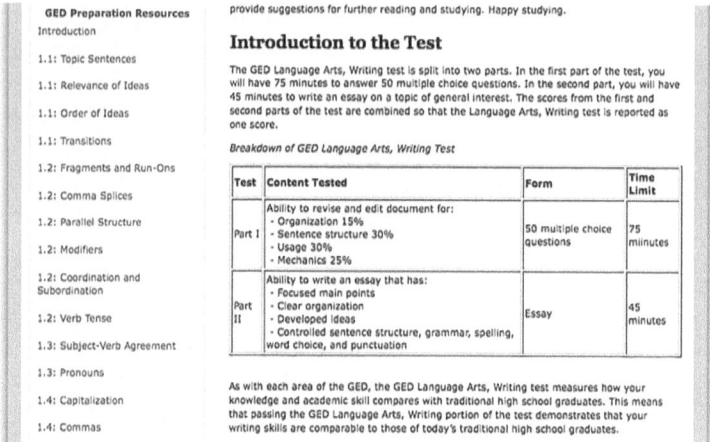

Figure 4.3 Original CWEST Taxonomy

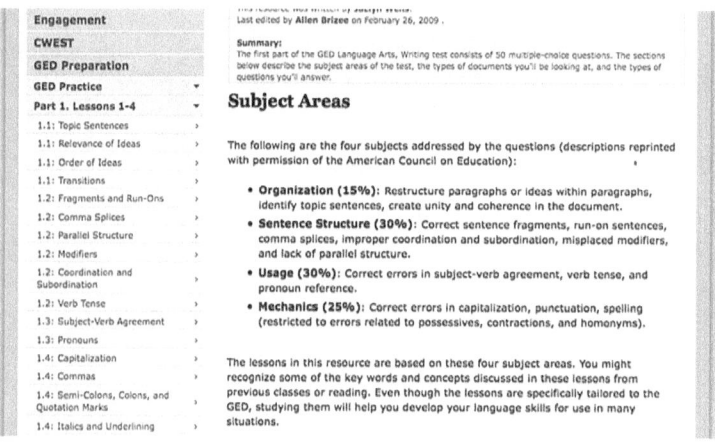

Figure 4.4 Revised CWEST Taxonomy

Moreover, only a few LARA teachers were actively using the CWEST. Though usability testing may have had the positive unexpected result of encouraging greater CWEST usage, the authors were still concerned that so few teachers were using the resources to begin with. One of the CWEST's primary measures of success was widespread adoption, and that adoption clearly was not happening. The findings thus far underscored the value of the iterative design process, which helped the authors as they moved into the WorkOne stage of the CWEST.

WORKING WITH WORKONE

Once Jaclyn and Allen had developed, posted, tested, and revised the LARA resources, they were ready to move into the WorkOne stage of the CWEST project. At this point, they recontacted the WorkOne coordinator, Sam, to organize an initial meeting and learn more about WorkOne's needs. Sam served as a research participant and helped Allen recruit other participants for the second stage of the CWEST project focused on job search documents. The following sections detail Allen's collaboration with WorkOne and the final stages of research for the CWEST project.

Meeting at the Sunrise Diner

Following a meeting with LARA administrators, Jaclyn and Allen walked over to the WorkOne lab to speak with Sam to arrange a meeting with him to discuss the next stage of the CWEST project. Sam stood behind his desk and scratched his chin.

"So." Long pause. "Have you eaten at the Sunrise Diner?" Sam asked.

Allen and Jaclyn hesitated for a second and eventually stammered at the same time, "Yes-No."

Jaclyn had eaten at the diner, but Allen hadn't. Though easily overlooked, the fact that Jaclyn had experienced one of Lafayette's best diners and Allen had not actually pointed to a disconnect. Sure, Allen had eaten at the Triple XXX Family Restaurant (featured on the Food Network's *Diners, Drive-Ins, and Dives*), but that student hangout is located in West Lafayette, the "Purdue side" of the Wabash River. He hadn't experienced local fare at the area's best diner, the Sunrise, located in downtown Lafayette.

Though Allen lived in Lafayette, the "town" side, he only visited downtown to eat at its few student-frequented restaurants or visit grad-school friends. Downtown was a place he drove through on the way to Purdue, across the South Street Bridge mentioned in chapter 2. So for all of the theory-based work on collaboration, and even with his background in service-learning and adult education, Allen was not as "local" as he would have liked.

Responding to Sam's confused look, Allen explained, "I guess Jaci's eaten there, but I haven't."

"Well, you need to," Sam said. "It's a great local place. And if you're trying to work with local people, you need to eat local. Let's meet there next Friday at 9 to talk more about your project. It's important to break bread together." After this quick conversation with Sam, the authors pushed open the WorkOne door and walked slowly down the hallway toward the LARA side of the Washington School building.

"Wow. That was embarrassing," Allen mumbled.

"It's okay, buddy," Jaclyn said. "Sunrise is a great place. Amazing biscuits and gravy. You'll love it."

In retrospect, Sam seemed to "get it," that is, "get" what the authors were trying to do with the CWEST project but in some ways not accomplishing. Allen had suggested meeting in the WorkOne lab, but Sam wanted to "break bread," as he put it, and meet in a local diner. Sam understood that as well intentioned as the authors were, they still had a lot to learn about the local community—Allen especially. During that first meeting at the Sunrise Diner, Jaclyn and Allen explained the project and the goal of fulfilling WorkOne's needs regarding job search resources. The most important information they learned was about the people who use WorkOne.

While the trio dined on delicious Sunrise biscuits and gravy, eggs and pancakes, Sam explained that WorkOne clients include people who must try to find employment as part of work release from the Tippecanoe County Correctional Facility. They are people who have been laid off after years of working for big companies in the area—Caterpillar, Wabash National, Subaru, Eli Lilly, and others, and they have families that need to eat and to buy clothes. These clients go to WorkOne to file for unemployment, to find jobs, and perhaps even to try to retrain and retool for the America's "new economy."

As the authors learned from Sam and from their demographic surveys, WorkOne clients represent a wide range of people struggling to survive the recession that crippled the already shaky manufacturing industry in the Midwest rust belt. WorkOne clients also come from the unstable agriculture industry: Struggling agribusiness plants had reduced their labor pool, thus throwing many immigrant workers out of jobs. In June 2009, approximately 31,977 out of a total 245,283 people (13.2 percent) in the area served by WorkOne were unemployed (Tippecanoe County and Indiana Region 4 Employment Data).

While discussing unemployment, Sam said, "WorkOne clients actually look a lot like the folks who come to the Sunrise Diner to eat and talk." Jaclyn and Allen glanced around the diner as Sam continued his explanation. In retrospect, it seems that Sam wanted to meet at the Sunrise to help reveal the human side of WorkOne clients outside the context that the authors had always experienced—the Washington School building.

Sam continued by saying that generally, WorkOne clients are of mixed ages, cultures, and language backgrounds (English and Spanish being the most prevalent), but that they reflect the demographics of the greater Lafayette area, excluding faculty and students at Purdue. Sam explained that many WorkOne clients have less experience with technology and writing than LARA learners but that some clients have completed their GEDs or finished ESL or high-school programs at LARA.

Sam also spoke about the connection between LARA and WorkOne and reminded the authors that while the two were separate entities, they helped many of the same people whose needs necessitated both of the programs. Sam commented that since the two organizations share a building, "it's easy for them [clients] to walk down the hall and get help finding a job at WorkOne." When Allen asked if this data was tracked, Sam responded, "Oh yes. We have to. LARA and WorkOne have to submit detailed yearly reports as part of our funding process." This comment again reminded the authors of their administrative work in the Purdue Writing Lab.

After this first breakfast meeting, Allen interviewed Sam throughout the project to work out the details of the WorkOne CWEST resources and review the research methods to be used to assess outcomes. Sam agreed to participate in the research and to help recruit more participants. One such participant, Sally, was a LARA volunteer who helped Sam during the week. She provided one of the most important findings in an interview with Allen when he asked about her definition of success at an interview in the WorkOne lab.

About project success, Sally commented:

> I would say if you have all this stuff in this room [the WorkOne lab] for them [clients] to use, to me success would be if 50% of them used it. To me that would be success because this clientele is transient, it's "I want you to sit with me forever," it's "well you're just mean, you don't want to help me," or "you're too old, you don't understand what I'm talking about." That's what we got here, so if I got 50% I would be happy.

Like Sally, Sam believed that usage and user satisfaction would indicate the project's success.

After these initial meetings and interviews, the WorkOne stage process began with observations at the WorkOne lab during various days and times. Similar to the LARA classroom, though smaller, the WorkOne lab offers a variety of workspaces. As overviewed in chapter 2, a visitor to the WorkOne lab will see people working at different tasks. The site coordinator or volunteer is either helping people with job searches or helping with computer work at the PCs lining the walls. Occasionally, the coordinator or volunteer will sit with clients at the tables to assist with job search material or to explain WorkOne services.

Once observations were complete, Allen collaborated with Sam to develop the job search resources. Once the drafts were posted, Allen conducted four usability tests and revised the job search resources based on data collected from those sessions. Therefore, the WorkOne stage of the CWEST generally replicated the iterative design process from the LARA stage: (1) conduct interviews and observations to develop resources; (2) post and test resources;

and (3) revise and repost resources. Additionally, Allen conducted a quasi-test, explained later in the chapter, during the last stage of CWEST work to help him evaluate outcomes of the WorkOne resources.

Technology Use at WorkOne

Based on the conversation with Sam at the Sunrise Diner, Allen's continuing conversations with him throughout the study, and demographic surveys, the authors knew that WorkOne clients had less experience with technology than LARA learners. While client ages were mixed, on average they were older than LARA learners, and their technology literacy was generally limited to surfing the Internet and basic MS Word use. Some WorkOne clients even had problems using the training software (Mavis Beacon Teaches Typing, ACT's KeyTrain, etc.) available in the WorkOne lab.

Sam explained students' lack of technology experience this way:

> I guess part of that is because so many of the people that come here are economically disadvantaged . . . they don't have a computer at home so the only time they see one is if they come here or go to the library.

For these reasons, many clients felt more comfortable with print resources, such as books and newspapers, than online resources for their job search and résumé writing.

In addition to inexperience with technology, most WorkOne clients did not have cover letters and did not foresee needing one. Clients focused on composing résumés using the template application, WinWay Resume Deluxe, available in the lab. Sam saw this as a problem because some employers required cover letters. After discussing needed resources with Sam, Allen decided to include letter-writing material to supplement the meager library of dusty and yellowing books.

Another challenge was WorkOne's lack of staffing. Sam only worked part time and could only assist one or two clients at a time, which frustrated people using the lab during busy hours. Though Sam held a graduate degree and had been the site coordinator for many years, he admitted that his skills with technology were "limited at best." While his skills were good enough to help people find job listings and compose basic résumés, Sam and the clients he helped were likely to be confused by the application process if online forms and submission systems were not as usable as they should have been.

Allen learned about the struggles of some of these WorkOne clients first hand when he spoke with a young woman, Amanda, who was trying to write a résumé and fill out online job applications. Amanda was a single parent (her daughter was with her), lacked a high-school diploma, and had limited technology skills. She knew how to navigate the Internet, but the poorly designed online applications proved frustrating and time consuming.

Despite her resolve, Amanda only filled out two applications in the hour she spent at WorkOne. Between her lack of recorded employment information and the slow going with the online forms, it took her thirty minutes to complete each application. Add to the mix the distraction of caring for a young child and the challenge of unusable online applications, and it's no wonder that Amanda's experience was frustrating and less productive than she wanted it to be. To Allen, Amanda's experience was an example of the connection between poverty, literacy, and usability.

Complicating the situation was the limited amount of time WorkOne volunteers from LARA had to assist people as the clients wrote their cover letters and résumés. Sally, the LARA volunteer mentioned previously, said: "Sometimes I will proofread . . . but we at WorkOne really don't have time to do the actual instruction. That's something they would do [at LARA], or they will have the skills when they come in."

In some ways, then, instruction at LARA aligned more closely with writing center pedagogy than did the support offered at WorkOne. At LARA, teachers sought to help students learn concepts and skills, while at WorkOne, teachers sought to help students achieve one specific goal (getting a job) with the skills they already had. But in situations like Amanda's, it was obvious that WorkOne users possessed limited literacy and technology skills that they might need to get those jobs. Because of these challenges, it was important to design the job search resources in an iterative fashion to ensure usability and to track the effectiveness of the work.

Results from Allen's observations at WorkOne illustrated the need for the CWEST project and its resources, because the Purdue OWL and other online resources were mostly geared for people with at least a high-school diploma and usually a college degree. Moreover, existing resources assumed that users would be composing job search documents using word processing programs on their own computers and printing them on their own printers. Most of the WorkOne clients did not own any of these expensive technologies.

Generally, the authors found that technology use among WorkOne clients fell into three main categories: (1) middle-aged or older adults: little or no technology experience; (2) middle-aged or older adults who had worked with technology in some capacity on the job: moderate technology experience but mainly with applications like Internet browsers, search engines, MS Office Suite, and email; and (3) younger adults on work release from prison: moderate technology experience but mainly with applications like Internet browsers, search engines, email, and social media.

The authors found that among WorkOne staff and volunteers, technology use fell into two major categories: (1) older adults: little or no technology experience and (2) middle-aged adults: moderate technology experience but mainly with applications like Internet browsers, search engines, job databases and applications, MS Word, and the software used in the lab, such as Mavis Beacon Teaches Typing, ACT's KeyTrain and WorkKeys, WinWay Resume Deluxe, and Rosetta Stone.

Developing the WorkOne Resources

The WorkOne pages were not as difficult to design as the LARA resources because the authors had already gone through the first generation of usability testing. Likewise, page content was not as difficult to compose due to the experience with LARA, so Allen was able to complete resources that were fairly usable from the start. Even more so than LARA students, WorkOne users sought efficient help that fit into their busy schedules, so they wanted very little text explanation for resources.

WorkOne interviews and observations pointed to three important findings that the authors took into the second generation of testing. First, as suggested previously, WorkOne differs from LARA in that people are focused on gaining employment instead of learning new concepts or skills. Second, writing instruction parallels this broader difference from LARA. As users seek help gaining employment with the skills they already have, writing instruction focuses on fixing problems rather than teaching new skills. Third, due to age and socioeconomic situation, most WorkOne users have less experience with technology than do LARA learners.

To address these unique aspects of all of WorkOne users' needs, Allen was guided by the two major questions:

1. How should he and Jaclyn adjust the design and composition process?
2. How should he and Jaclyn adjust the testing and revision process?

From the observations, Allen gleaned a lot of important information that spoke to these two questions and helped the authors revise the WorkOne resources' design and testing.

Most importantly, the authors learned from Allen's observations that the resources needed to be tailored for all users at WorkOne. For clients and staff, the resources had to be usable, both in terms of navigation and prose. For clients, the material had to reflect their life situations, such as applying for jobs at fast food restaurants, grounds keeping, and janitorial companies. For staff, the resources needed to be usable and understandable so that they could help users quickly when the lab got busy. On the other hand, the resources needed to be robust enough to be used for cover letter and résumé workshops.

To respond to these needs, Allen composed the following resources with the WorkOne participants. Each category listed below contained multiple resources and document samples posted in PDF for easy download and printing.

- Reading and Using Job Ads
- Job Applications
- Résumés
- Cover Letters
- Interviews
- Follow-Up and Thank You Letters

GENERATION TWO TESTING

To meet the challenges outlined above, Allen followed an iterative design process similar to the approach the authors used with LARA. Though he did not run focus groups, Allen did work closely with Sam and Sally, the site coordinator and LARA volunteer discussed throughout this chapter (Sally also participated in the first test session). He also worked closely with two WorkOne end users (both females) and two human resource experts (one male and one female). Since the research methods are already outlined above, the authors provide only an overview of the test two session and its results below.

In keeping with the iterative, participatory design process used for the first test session, the authors began by recruiting participants and getting their feedback on the project's approach and how they would define success for the CWEST. Next, the authors worked closely with the WorkOne participants to draft the job analysis, cover letter and résumé, and job interview resources.

Next, Jaclyn and Allen posted and tested the resources following the protocols outlined above. Direct comparisons with first test session results could not be made, however, because the authors had revised the CWEST area of the Purdue OWL, the authors were testing different resources, and they were working with different participants. Finally, the authors revised the resources again before posting the final drafts on the Purdue OWL in the Engagement section. The flowchart at figure 4.5 illustrates this process.

As illustrated in figure 4.5, the WorkOne stage of the CWEST added a step in the research process, the quasi-experiment (see the findings section for a fuller discussion).

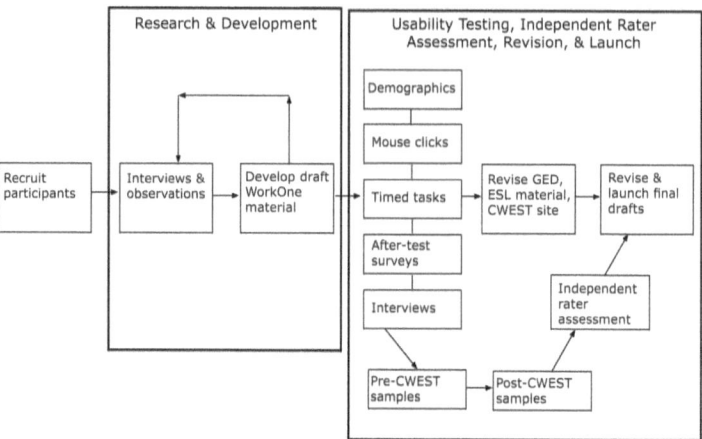

Figure 4.5   CWEST Generation 2 Testing

Usability Findings

For the second test session, participants took between 80.83 and 215.67 seconds (mean: 157.11) to complete the three tasks (the fourth task was speak aloud, so the authors did not collect data on mouse clicks or time to complete task). Participants used between 3 and 7.17 (mean: 4.6) mouse clicks to complete the tasks, and participants completed 83 percent of the tasks. In short, the usability of the resources improved slightly following revisions from the first round of testing, but Allen and Jaclyn still had more work to do.

Like the first round of tests, the trend of increasing or mixed results for time to complete task and number of mouse clicks continued. With the exception of the second task, participants took longer to find information and used more mouse clicks. Also, the number of tasks completed decreased throughout the test. In the second round, participants' time to complete tasks and mouse clicks used to find information increased. Tasks completed also decreased, but they improved from the first session (60 percent) to the second (83 percent). Moreover, the number of mouse clicks increased from the first to the second session, but the time to complete tasks decreased.

Observing participant navigation paths, the authors determined that the increased times and mouse clicks were probably due to the increase in navigation options and resources from the first round to the second round—participants simply had more choices because of the addition of WorkOne materials to the GED and ESL resources. Regardless of improvements in some areas, the test two results indicated lingering problems with usability. The post-test surveys and interviews confirmed this idea.

The second round post-test feedback methods mirrored those from the first round. While survey results showed that participants did not find the website and resources unusable, the overall scores indicated that more work was needed to fulfill the community partners' needs. On a 1–5 scale, participant total average impression scored a 3.75, which was a 0.70 improvement from the 3.05 rating from the first session. But as a "very high neutral," the 3.75 score was still not the positive result that Jaclyn and Allen wanted.

The second round post-test interviews provided insight into how the WorkOne resources could be improved. The interviews also reinforced the authors' belief that the navigation and resources had improved from round one (the LARA stage) to round two (the WorkOne stage). The interviews suggested that the wording of the WorkOne resources remained difficult. One participant, Sally, explained the text-heavy pages in this way: "So I think for the staff the resource would be very helpful. For the user, I don't know. I think . . . I put on my comment sheet that it looks intimidating."

To help address the text-heavy appearance of the materials, participants suggested reducing word count, increasing text size, and adding visuals. Even though previous findings suggested the same about LARA resources, and even though the authors revised resources based on those findings, Allen still ran into the same problems with the WorkOne material. Based on all of these new suggestions, the authors further simplified the wording, increased text size, and added presentation slides to increase visual aids for the WorkOne resources.

Improving Writing

As noted above, helping WorkOne users improve their writing was especially difficult because people come to WorkOne for employment, not to improve their composition skills. The writing instruction that occurs at WorkOne is prescriptive, focused, and intense; it differs greatly from instruction at LARA or Purdue's Writing Lab. Due to the prescriptive nature of the writing instruction, work on cover letters can be abrupt. Staff members do not have the time to explain the finer nuances of rhetorical theory and reader-centered prose. Allen tried to address this challenge by using reader-centered strategies presented in skill-level-appropriate ways.

These points drove the authors' work as they discussed how to measure participants' writing improvement. Given that WorkOne's context differed so markedly from LARA, the Writing Lab, and other, more familiar places, the authors struggled with how to assess the participants' writing. Allen asked a LARA administrator with experience in education assessment about measuring outcomes of the cover letter and résumé resources. She responded by saying: "I think, ideally, the best measurement is some kind of pre-measure and post-measure, but that is pretty ideal."[3] This comment supported doing a quasi-experiment.

To determine whether or not WorkOne resources were helping end users improve their writing, two WorkOne participants submitted résumés and cover letters before and after using the job search materials to revise their documents. Allen submitted these documents to two independent raters for assessment.[4] Assessment rubrics for the résumés and cover letters were designed based on professional writing scholarship, best practices, and personal experience.[5]

Further, the rubrics were split into two overall categories: Design and Content. Design subcategories included Appearance and Layout, while the Content subcategories included the typical sections found in these documents: Objective, Education, Introduction, Body Paragraphs, Conclusion, etc. The raters also assessed the applicant's professional qualifications and recorded whether or not they would interview them. Allen averaged the two raters' scores to render results and averaged the score of all seven categories to render the raters' overall "Impression" of the applicant.

The independent raters reported that WorkOne participant 1, Karen, improved her résumé in all but one category, Appearance (this score remained the same). The raters also considered Karen more qualified as a potential interviewee and had a more favorable impression of her after she revised her résumé using the WorkOne resources. The raters reported that in all but one category, Appearance (this score remained the same), Karen improved her cover letter. Raters also considered Karen more qualified and had a more favorable impression of her after reading her revision.

For participant 2, Beth, raters reported that the résumé was improved in all but two categories, Experience and References (these scores remained the same). The raters also considered Beth more qualified as a potential interviewee and had a more favorable impression of her after she revised her résumé. Raters reported that in all but three categories, Appearance, Layout, and Address (these scores remained the same), Beth improved her cover letter after using the WorkOne resources. The raters also considered Beth more qualified as a potential interviewee and had a more favorable impression of her after reading her revision.

These findings indicate that in all but a few categories the independent raters reported improvements, some of them marked, in Karen's and Beth's revised résumés and cover letters. Improvements in the documents had a dramatic effect on raters' impressions of the applicants. Both raters responded that their impressions of Karen and Beth improved and that their opinion of applicants' qualifications improved. Moreover, the raters reported that their likelihood of interviewing Karen and Beth increased after reading the revised cover letters and résumés.

Though the CWEST project to this point had assisted some of the participants, and the community partners seemed pleased, Allen and Jaclyn resisted the urge to proclaim success. In some ways, the project had gone well, but in others, it had fallen short. The authors experienced some serious challenges and limitations—the messy parts of the project—that are important to discuss for scholars interested in conducting similar work. The next chapter details this information and provides Jaclyn and Allen's reflections on their individual experiences with the CWEST.

NOTES

1. A. Brizee (2014). "Toward Participatory Civic Engagement: Findings and Implications of a Three-year Community-based Research Study," *Computers and Composition: An International Journal 32*, 22–40.

2. It is possible that participants' speak-aloud requirements for question 4 could have influenced their ability to find the correct information.

3. This mirrors the writing assessment research design Allen used to measure outcomes of participants using the CWEST to revise their cover letters and résumés.

4. Allen did not pretrain the raters because they were already skilled human resource professionals, and Allen did not test for inter-rater reliability due to the number of participants ($n = 2$) and number of assessors ($n = 2$).

5. Allen has worked as a technical writer for the federal government and as an independent contractor, and he also collected data for these categories during an interview with a hiring representative from U.S. Steel during a Purdue campus job fair.

Chapter 5

Discussion and Key Takeaways

In service-learning, instructors regularly ask students to reflect on their work and constantly raise questions to elicit that reflection. What did you learn? What aspects of your work were more and less successful? What might you do differently next time? How might you apply what you learned to future personal, professional, or civic situations? Jaclyn and Allen argue that when university members engage the community, they must ask themselves similar questions.

The reasons for such questioning are many. Most importantly, even for a very seasoned community engagement leader and researcher, community-based experiences will raise new challenges and present new lessons. Approaching experiences with an attitude of openness and curiosity will, as Flower (2008) suggested, make the most of knowledge-making opportunities and help cultivate better relationships with community members.

Taking this approach may have felt more natural to the authors, since both were students when the CWEST project began. As they worked toward finishing their degrees, Allen and Jaclyn learned about community-based research and engagement and all they both entail while collaborating with LARA and WorkOne. During many parts of the project, the authors stumbled, made mistakes, and learned lessons that could inform the project itself and their future work as researchers, administrators, teachers, and community leaders.

In this chapter, the authors discuss in separate sections the limitations and even the failures of the CWEST project, not to berate themselves or disparage the work, but to provide readers with some of the most important information generated by the CWEST: what was learned from the project that may help others interested in doing similar work with their communities. In doing so,

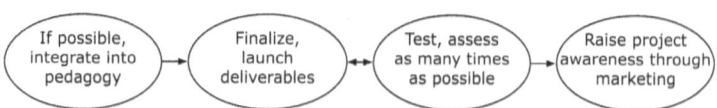

Figure 5.1   Final Steps

the chapter covers information from the last four steps, shown in figure 5.1, of the model presented in its entirety in chapter 1.

JACLYN'S REFLECTIONS

In chapter 1, Jaclyn reflects on her path through education. She describes feeling regularly out of place or left behind, especially in college and graduate school, as though she had missed some crucial information or lesson. Much of that feeling stemmed from issues of class and the resulting lack of experiences like traveling. Despite these feelings, there is no denying that Jaclyn's route through education was nearly as traditional as possible. Before the CWEST project, she had never experienced a nontraditional learning environment, either as a teacher, tutor, or student.

Jaclyn came to the CWEST project with the sense that she knew more than she did about community contexts like LARA and WorkOne, mainly because she overestimated how much her off-campus socialization would contribute and underestimated how much she needed to learn about nontraditional educational settings. On the one hand, Jaclyn expected to feel comfortable around the community participants, and she was. On the other, Jaclyn and Allen needed more than simply feeling comfortable interacting with the community partners.

In part, Jaclyn's comfort level came from how much she knew about the *community*. She came to the project aware that the Sunrise Diner offered the best biscuits and gravy in Lafayette, a kind of knowledge that is easy to overlook but important nonetheless. However, Jaclyn did not know much about the community *partner* (or other organizations like them). Her limited experience of nontraditional educational settings and students influenced her view of school and her early work in the CWEST, and she had to learn about environments like LARA to contribute more effectively.

Writing for a New Teaching Context

The first drafts of CWEST GED materials were densely packed with information. Everything was *long*: long sentences, long paragraphs, long sections.

When drafting the first round of GED resources, Jaclyn underestimated how much LARA students needed readable, usable materials because she imagined the same classroom setup that she had experienced as a student and teacher. While many of Jaclyn's own teaching materials could almost certainly have been clearer, explaining them during class time allowed her to address students' confusion.

Jaclyn learned from observation that instruction at LARA differs greatly from this traditional setup, so that instructors do not always have the opportunity to go over confusing, unwieldy handouts with students. This situation means that clear, readable materials are crucial. Additionally, many LARA students lacked confidence from not succeeding in traditional learning environments, which further necessitated accessible materials that do not frustrate. This characteristic in the student population marks another difference from environments where Jaclyn had studied and taught.

To develop appropriate GED materials, Jaclyn had to learn about LARA's teaching context instead of drawing on her own teaching experience in the university. LARA's individualized, student-centered approach more closely resembled Jaclyn's work in the writing center than her work in the first-year composition or professional writing classroom. This was useful, as Jaclyn could partly draw on her work in the writing center, where the one-on-one approach had some similarity to LARA's attention to individual needs, goals, and preferred learning strategies.

Still, a typical day in LARA's learning lab differs even from a typical day in the writing center. In the learning lab, teachers help students set an agenda for independent study and check in regularly while they work. This differs greatly from most writing centers, like the Purdue Writing Lab, where tutors sit down one-on-one with students for a specific amount of time (usually thirty or sixty minutes). As participant Ann described, LARA teachers often act as "maître'd's who 'serve education up' to students," so the teachers need clear materials they can assign for independent study.

Learning more about LARA's teaching context helped Jaclyn to revise the materials to better support instruction. Once materials were broken down into smaller, more digestible sections of text, they were far more compatible with LARA's teaching context and student population. Others working with a community literacy program should learn about the program's teaching context and understand that it will likely differ greatly from university contexts; further, others interested in developing teaching materials should know that these differences in context will affect their resources.

Including a research component in engagement projects will help university partners to better understand the community literacy context and help prevent assumptions or overreliance on the university members' own teaching experience, experience that may be irrelevant to adult literacy instruction. Further, as the CWEST illustrates, this research must be more than a one-shot deal. Jaclyn *had* researched LARA before creating the first round of resources—and this research no doubt worked toward stronger first drafts—but further research enabled necessary revisions.

"Real" Research in Action

Because Jaclyn genuinely needed to know about LARA's teaching context to create and revise the GED materials, research about LARA was about as real as it gets. In other words, the authors were not raising research questions in a theoretical sense, but rather, raising questions they actually needed to answer to proceed in the engagement work. What Jaclyn was doing in researching LARA during the GED phase of the CWEST, though she did not realize it when the project began, was action research.

In "Reconstructing the Relationships between Universities and Society through Action Research" (2003), Greenwood and Levin propose action research as a method of creating knowledge that is both contextual and applicable to real problems. Action research is particularly useful, they argue, in repairing the relationship between the public and university, a relationship that has long been damaged by the university's lack of attention to public concerns.

Greenwood and Levin (2003) argue that collaboration with local stakeholders allows action researchers to build the type of knowledge required to produce action. The reason is "Only *local stakeholders*, with their years of experience in a particular situation, have sufficient information and knowledge about the situation to design effective *social change processes*" [emphasis added] (p. 150). Greenwood and Levin make clear that if researchers want to produce real action, they need to be open to collaboration with other stakeholders who can share the knowledge necessary to making that action happen.

In the CWEST project, these local stakeholders were the LARA instructors, who were able to teach the authors about adult literacy. When the project began, Jaclyn would have described the social change process in this collaboration simply in local terms, perhaps saying something like, "our goal is to bring together educators of different levels in the Lafayette area." As the project progressed, Jaclyn realized that she, Allen, and the community partners were attempting a much larger social change by creating a model for collaboration among teachers in the university and community literacy contexts.

Additionally, the CWEST partners were attempting to support adult education nationwide by providing free study materials via the Purdue OWL. Since many adult students, like those who study at LARA and WorkOne, deal with issues of poverty, unemployment, and lack of educational access, the work supported even broader social change by providing adult students free resources to support goals like passing the GED and gaining employment.

Further, as Mike Rose described in *Back to School* (2012), nontraditional students and "second-chance institutions" like LARA and WorkOne are sometimes overlooked in larger conversations about education, as is evidenced by the OWL's lack of adult education materials. Bringing adult literacy education into the Purdue OWL represented a small but critical step toward increasing national attention to this group of students and educators.

However, the current placement of the CWEST resources on the OWL represents both the limitations and the necessity for university-community collaborations. This current placement illustrates that collaborations like the one Allen and Jaclyn shared with LARA and WorkOne will face challenges beyond the university and community partners' control. Neither the authors nor the LARA/WorkOne teachers could control the GED exam's 2012 revision, which made the CWEST GED materials outdated and necessitated their removal from the OWL (see the epilogue for more discussion on this).

While this certainly felt discouraging, the reality of the GED test acquisition serves as an important reminder that community-based research and engagement always happen within larger contexts, in this case, the broader national context of GED testing. To create real social change, even a three-year project like the CWEST is inadequate. Instead, many community-university partnerships must *keep doing the work.* The CWEST's limitations do not prove community engagement's failures; rather, they show that community engagement projects must be many rather than isolated incidents.

Researcher as Engaged Participant

As Greenwood and Levin's (2003) discussion suggests, action research calls for a collaborative relationship between researcher and research participant. To collaborate with local stakeholders in the ways Greenwood and Levin proposed, university researchers may need to shift their perceptions of their role. When the authors began research with LARA, Jaclyn quickly realized a flawed perspective she did not even know she held: the image of the Researcher.

The Researcher, Jaclyn thought, maintained an unemotional, unbiased, and unengaged presence; she was the quintessential fly-on-the-wall observing reality from afar before bringing her notes and her recordings back to the office for analysis and write-up. When the authors began research, Jaclyn learned quickly that community-based scholars differ greatly from the image of researcher she had in mind.

In particular, Jaclyn learned that the idea of the objective, detached researcher is simply unrealistic when collaborating with community partners and seeking information that will directly inform an engagement project. Researching *with* the community and *about* an engagement project, she learned, demands a very different approach. Attempting to maintain an objective, unengaged presence can damage the very relationship community-based research and engagement seek to establish.

Jaclyn's idea of the Researcher stemmed in part from the examples of academic research she had encountered, many of which did not follow the collaborative, action-focused orientation that community-based research demands. Greenwood and Levin (2003) also speak to the scarcity of collaborative, action-focused research and the abundance of its opposite. They suggest that university social science researchers have often failed to conduct research that has value for the world outside the academy, thus neglecting to contribute to the very public that often supports this research.

Many academic social scientists, Greenwood and Levin (2003) proposed, "show a lack of concern with the application of the results of their work or reject such application outright, arguing either that connections to the world beyond the university invade their intellectual autonomy or . . . threaten their 'objectivity'" (p. 133). While this may allow for a degree of intellectual freedom, it also creates "useless research and academic careerism divorced from attention to important public social issues" (p. 136).

In particular, those who (rightly, as Greenwood and Levin [2003] suggested) expect university research to address important public issues will be disappointed by the exclusive focus that prevails throughout much academic scholarship. But, not all are ignored equally: Greenwood and Levin argued that university research consistently ignores particular groups, such as "small-scale organizations, minorities, and other powerless or poor people who want assistance with broad social change issues" (p. 138). The authors argue that this includes programs like LARA and WorkOne.

Jaclyn's teaching observations most dramatically shifted her thinking about researcher engagement. As described in previous chapters, she observed teaching before and after the GED preparation materials had been launched. In the first round of observations, Jaclyn hoped to gather insights that would inform development of the GED materials, and in the second round, she hoped to gather information that would inform the materials' revision.

Although observations did indeed prove valuable for gathering this information about how to revise CWEST materials, Jaclyn's original vision of what those observations would look like—sitting quietly, watching objectively, taking notes furiously—was off. As her perspective was shaped by common examples of academic research, many newcomers to community-based research may share this original vision.

Jaclyn's very first observation illustrates how the reality of community-based action research conflicted with her original image of the Researcher.

For this first observation, Jaclyn arrived at LARA with pen and notebook in hand. After signing in at the front desk, she made her way to the learning lab and greeted the teacher she would observe that day, Susan. Susan said to take a seat anywhere. Jaclyn settled in the back of the room, trying to remain unobtrusive. Despite these efforts, she felt as though she wore a sign that read, "Graduate student from across the river."

Jaclyn receded into the background once the action began, and she watched as the participants' restaurant and sports metaphors for their teaching came to life. Susan appeared as a maître d' of education in initial conversations with many students; she negotiated with students what they would study that day and then "served up" the materials and a loose plan for their time. She resembled a basketball player at other points, first playing "a zone" by checking in with part of the classroom and then quickly switching to "man-to-man" when she spotted a student who needed one-on-one attention.

For the first half of the observation, Jaclyn sat in silence, furiously taking notes on everything. Toward the middle of the session, she observed a student growing frustrated writing a paragraph in MS Word, but from where she sat, could not see the source of the student's frustration. Even after observing this frustration, Jaclyn remained seated and clung to the outside-observer role. Eventually, Susan called her over to help. Jaclyn nervously approached, worried about breaking out of the observer role even when invited.

As Jaclyn greeted the student, she mimicked the friendly, "we're-in-this-together" tone she used in the writing center. "Hey," she said. "What's giving you trouble?"

The student gestured toward the computer and replied, "It keeps deleting everything I write."

Jaclyn looked over the student's shoulder and immediately understood the problem. The student was attempting to insert a new sentence in the middle of her paragraph, but she had accidentally switched to "overwrite" mode in MS Word, so that all of the new text would delete the old instead of simply shoving it over, like in the program's default setting.

Jaclyn remembered her frustration when this had happened as she was learning to use MS Word in college. Again, she drew on her experience in the writing center, where she often related to students by sharing her own experiences.

"It's so easy to turn overwrite mode on by accident," she said. "I remember the first time it happened to me, and it about drove me crazy before I finally figured out how to turn it back off." Jaclyn quickly showed the student how to turn off overwrite mode, turned three shades of red when Susan praised her for being a "technology whiz," and shuffled back to her seat.

Similar moments happened throughout all of the first-round observations. Jaclyn spent most of the observations sitting and watching, but during every one, she was approached at least once to weigh in or pitch in. Refusing to engage would have been more than awkward or impolite. Without engaging when invited, Jaclyn would have missed significant opportunities to better understand LARA, its teachers, and its students.

While it can feel uncomfortable to suddenly switch from research to engagement mode, researchers can make this move more comfortable by remembering that to research the community is to engage the community, and vice versa. Just as research can contribute to engagement projects, participating when invited can improve the quality of information gathered about the community. Had Jaclyn refused to engage with students or ignored how the findings could improve the project, she risked succumbing to the type of antiapplication research that Greenwood and Levin (2003) describe.

Taking a Flexible, Open Approach

Jaclyn's observation at LARA's jail branch best exemplifies how expectations for research sometimes conflicted with reality. Here, she was asked to engage more than during any of the other observations; had she hesitated to step out of the comfortable observer role, Jaclyn would have missed opportunities for understanding and contributing that were opened by participating. Additionally, the jail observation simultaneously provides a good example of how much Jaclyn had to learn about nontraditional education settings and how some of her teaching and tutoring experiences did translate.

Jaclyn observed Betty, a longtime LARA instructor who had taught the GED classes in the jail for many years. In the jail parking lot, she met Betty, who quickly reminded Jaclyn of the rules for entering. Most important among them: absolutely no pencil sharpeners or ink pens. Prepared with a notebook and freshly sharpened No. 2 pencil, Jaclyn followed Betty nervously into the jail.

When the students walked into the classroom, Jaclyn realized immediately how silly her nervousness had been. She and Betty were entering a county jail, not a maximum-security prison. Most of the offenders were there on drug charges, and very few were jailed for violent crimes. Though Jaclyn knew this consciously, she still had TV images of filthy prisons and hardened prisoners. But the students were mainly Jaclyn's age or younger, quiet, and respectful, and the jail classroom was clean and bright.

Jaclyn spent the first part of the observation simply watching, assuming that fly-on-the-wall researcher role that she had imagined before beginning research at LARA. The first part of day's work closely resembled a traditional class and contrasted with the LARA learning lab, where all students were working on different topics during individual study. Betty passed out handouts, lectured the group of students for a bit, and then asked for responses to questions. In the second half of the session, students worked independently on the same general topic, the essay portion of the GED exam.

During the second half of the GED class, Jaclyn became involved. Betty asked her to show some students the GED Essay Game, which the authors had saved for her on CDs, since the jail classroom had computers but no Internet access (see chapter 3 for more information on the GED game). Betty expressed enthusiasm when the authors introduced her to the game, but during the classroom observation at the jail, Jaclyn learned that she had not yet used it with students.

Betty explained during the observation that she had been waiting for *Jaclyn* to show the students how to use the game. This reveals one limitation of the project that was based on a breakdown of communication and a difference in expectations. For all of their discussion of the project's complex nature, the authors still sometimes viewed their role and the timeline for work as fairly straightforward. For Jaclyn, the timeline was: (1) study LARA; (2) develop drafts of instructional materials for GED preparation; (3) observe the materials in use; and (4) revise according to the findings.

Initially, Jaclyn believed (not entirely consciously) that her role revolved almost entirely around the materials themselves; while she would talk to instructors and observe their teaching, she believed that work would focus on how to improve the materials. From Betty's perspective, though, it made little sense for Jaclyn to visit the jail branch to merely observe the action. Further, it made little sense for *her* to introduce the materials to the students, since Jaclyn would be visiting the classroom anyway.

Further, Betty viewed Jaclyn as the expert when it came to digital instructional materials, even though she had taught for over two decades and expressed enthusiasm and expertise with the Internet and technology. Finally, even after learning about the students and witnessing firsthand that many of them feared technology, Jaclyn still underestimated how much instruction some of them would require before using materials like the GED Essay Game; she had assumed (again, not entirely consciously) that introducing the game would just involve Betty's showing it to them.

When Betty asked her to help a group of students write practice essays using the game, Jaclyn needed to switch quickly from observer to tutor. Fortunately, Jaclyn's experience in the writing center helped her move fairly comfortably into this role; though the context of a jail-based GED classroom clearly differs from a university writing center, she was being called to use similar skills during the observation of Betty's class. For example, Jaclyn negotiated the agenda and asked questions following a similar process that tutors might use in a writing center session.

In the writing center, Jaclyn focused almost entirely on writing while setting the agenda with students. Knowing that many LARA students had limited experience with technology, she included questions about experience with computers when she sat down to show Betty's students the GED Essay Game. Still, in both situations, Jaclyn attempted to engage the students in conversation, understand their level and needs, and tailor her support accordingly.

"Hey!" Jaclyn began with one student. "Have you used anything like the GED Game before?" The student replied that he had not, and she asked, "Have you drafted any GED practice essays before, like just using pen and paper?"

"I have written a couple," he replied. "We've been working on it in here for the past couple weeks."

Jaclyn asked next about the student's experience with technology, and it turned out that he was one of the students who preferred working on the computer. Jaclyn showed him the game, and he spent the rest of the session diligently prewriting, drafting, and revising an essay using it.

This example illustrates the need for flexibility in community-based research, where the line between researcher and participant very often blurs. It also illustrates that even though university participants cannot rely exclusively on their experiences teaching and tutoring in the university context, drawing on these experiences may be valuable. Perhaps the best university participants can do is to avoid assuming that their experiences translate, instead entering the community with the goal of learning from the community partner first.

ALLEN'S REFLECTIONS

Like Jaclyn's journey, Allen's path through education was filled with awkwardness and feelings of disconnect. Less a class issue and more a mixture of immaturity and limited institutional flexibility, Allen's stumbling journey through high school led him to the last-chance net referred to in previous chapters—the Bryant Adult Education Center. Bryant was established by the public school system to catch people like Allen, people who hadn't succeeded on the traditional path.

For many years, Allen blamed the public school system for failing him rather than accepting personal responsibility for his tumble out of two traditional high schools. But after rushing to this conclusion and then shoving Bryant into the dark corners of his memory, Allen slowly began to realize that Bryant didn't represent his failure, it just represented a *different* path. This different path enabled Allen to try for a third time to earn a diploma and scramble toward more education and a better life.

This realization was slow to form. When Allen began Purdue's PhD program, he at least considered Bryant a part of his success story rather than a mark of failure. He didn't want to discuss it, but didn't avoid it if people asked. When the CWEST project evolved into a formative part of Allen's PhD program, it became clear that his experience at Bryant would not merely be a stepping stone to higher degrees and an academic career; rather, it occurred to him that Bryant was actually a transformative experience that would influence his life as an activist scholar.

In many ways, Allen's time at Bryant allowed him to feel at home at LARA in some of the same ways that Jaclyn felt at home in Lafayette. He felt comfortable walking through the hallways of the Washington School building, an adopted home for LARA, because it was like walking the hallways of the Bryant building, which had originally been home to another school.

Even before Allen shared his stories about Bryant with the folks at LARA, he felt as if he knew a lot about them, and he felt a part of their world. Though in some ways, upon reflection, Allen thinks that this feeling was a bit naïve; nevertheless, his different journey through high school that ended at Bryant did allow him to feel more at ease while collaborating with LARA and WorkOne.

However, some of these feelings were overconfidence that may have contributed to some of the early blunders the authors experienced with the CWEST. Even though Allen knew something about adult education, what he didn't realize during the CWEST project was that his experience with non-traditional education at Bryant came at a time when he was different, when he knew less and experienced life in a less mature manner. Just because he had been a student at Bryant didn't mean that he was somehow an expert in adult education or community-based research, as the following example illustrates.

Sometimes, You Break Things

Jaclyn and Allen were both very nervous, even though they had thoroughly prepared for this day—the first day of usability testing on the LARA GED resources. Allen had run through the protocols numerous times (they were very similar to the ones used for the Purdue OWL usability project); Jaclyn had read and re-read the post-test interview questions; and the LARA administrators had reserved a small, quiet office with a computer so the authors could conduct the tests away from the hustle of daily LARA activity.

The authors had set up two audio-recording devices, and the data-recording sheets were neatly stacked next to the computer where the participant would sit. Allen was to proctor the test while Jaclyn noted navigation paths.

Dana Driscoll, who was assisting with this first test, would record how long it took for the participant to complete tasks and count mouse clicks. All in all, it was a tight fit in the small office.

As the participant walked in and sat down, everyone engaged in pleasant small talk, and the conversation slowly shifted to the CWEST project. After providing a brief explanation (she was a LARA teacher and so knew most of the details), the authors explained the informed consent document. Once she read and signed the form, Allen reviewed the process, saying that the test and the post-test survey and interview would take about an hour. She nodded her head, and Jaclyn sat next to her.

Allen began: "Jaclyn and Dana are going to observe you using the computer and the website while I ask you to find information in the resources. Remember that we're not testing *your* ability with the computer or the Internet, rather we're testing the resources and then getting your feedback on how you feel about them. If that's ok, we'll get started."

"Sure, that's fine," she replied. Jaclyn and Dana settled in and prepared the data-recording sheets while Allen began the questions.

That's when it happened. Allen leaned on the fiberboard desktop holding an aging bubble jet printer. The desktop creaked and then crashed to the floor, sending him flailing against the wall. Allen dropped his pen and test protocols and almost fell on the broken desk. Startled, everyone in the room jumped and stared at him as he struggled to regain his composure, collect his materials, and reassemble the desk, all at the same time. An administrator from the next office ran in.

"Is everything ok? I heard a big crash," she said.

Mortified, Allen turned and replied, "Um, yeah, we're fine. I broke the desk when I leaned on it. We'll pay to replace it and the printer if that's broken." He struggled to lift the desk and printer off the floor.

The LARA administrator said, "That's ok. Just leave it. It doesn't look too bad. I'll have our maintenance guy look at it later."

"Are you sure?" Allen stammered.

"Really, it's fine. Finish your testing." Mortified, Allen asked the participant if she would like to continue. She said she was fine.

Allen glanced at Jaclyn, who seemed astonished and horrified. Dana was trying not to laugh as she hid her face behind one of the data-collection sheets. After settling in, the authors ran through the protocols, asked the participant to complete the after-test survey, and conducted the after-test interview. The rest of the session went well, and the participant enjoyed working with the resources and providing feedback.

At the time, Allen thought that he had just made an unforgivable mistake. As the research participant left the office, he told Jaclyn and Dana, "I can't believe I did that. I'm such a klutz."

Dana replied, "Well Allen, your heart's in the right place, but sometimes you break things." The more Allen reflected on this incident, the more it reminded him of the failed service-learning projects the authors had read about for the literature review in the original proposal from Patricia Sullivan's public rhetorics course.

In such projects, instructors and students had begun work with the best intentions, but somehow, the project had either fizzled or had dramatically gone down in flames: community partners arguing with students at a neighborhood meeting, deliverables being sent to organizations in file formats they couldn't use. Between the lackluster responses from the focus groups and Allen's unfortunate incident with the desk, he worried that he and Jaclyn had begun such a project—entering with good intentions but, in fact, just breaking things.

When the authors returned for the second test the following week, Allen asked about the desk and the printer. The LARA administrator said, "They're fine. We have a great maintenance guy. He's used to fixing busted things around here. We don't have the money to buy new." Sure enough, when the authors walked into the office to set up the equipment and lay out their forms, the desk was repaired, and the printer looked fine.

For Allen, that repair illustrated how LARA/WorkOne sometimes had to accomplish tasks; folks didn't get too stressed. They just figured out how to overcome adversity and fixed things to make them work. Thankfully, the rest of the LARA test sessions were uneventful. However, Allen continued to reflect on this experience as a metaphor for how quickly things can spiral out of control or go wrong when university members step off campus and into the local community. Even when we're careful, we can break things.

Inherent Challenges to Community-Based Research

Aside from early setbacks of the desk-breaking nature, the authors faced other common challenges and limitations related to civic engagement and research. One inherent challenge to community-based research that they encountered included the limited number of end-user participants for the usability tests and the limited number of WorkOne participants who submitted pre- and post-writing resource use documents.

Though scholarship indicates that effective usability research is possible with eleven (the first test session included thirteen) or fewer participants (session two involved four participants with one testing in both sessions one and two) (Coe, 1996; Hwang and Salvendy, 2010), Allen wanted to recruit more end-user participants from LARA and WorkOne to obtain more data.

However, recruiting and retaining participants from this at-risk population was challenging. For example, some WorkOne participants showed up for the second round of usability tests but then neglected to submit cover letters and résumés. One participant only submitted a draft cover letter and résumé but did not return for the usability test and did not submit revisions. The authors were able to work with a satisfactory number of administrators, teachers, and volunteers, but they felt that more end-user participants were needed.

Other possible limitations to the research portion of the CWEST project include the Hawthorne and Reverse Hawthorne Effects. These limitations are risks in many study settings with many types of populations, but can be more risky in community-based research. The Hawthorne Effect is, essentially, the phenomenon whereby research participants improve work processes because they know they are in an observational or test setting. The Reverse Hawthorne Effect is the opposite: participants' performance on tasks decreases because they know they are part of a study.

The authors had one participant who self-reported test anxiety during the usability sessions, and her time-on task and mouse clicks were far higher than those of other participants. In the end, the authors chose not to remove this outlier from the statistical data even though her scores fell far above two standard deviations of the mean. They kept the data because they felt it represented an important aspect of the entire set.

The Halo and Subject and Research Expectancy Effects present other possible challenges. The Halo Effect is the phenomenon whereby participants' feedback is skewed by their positive relationship with researchers, and Subject and Research Expectancy Effects impact data due to high expectations of the research project itself. Both of these are particularly difficult to control for in civic engagement projects because activist researchers and their students are *trying* to build positive relationships with their community partners—it's part of the point of doing the projects in the first place.

Additionally, participants *want* the project to succeed, so they might respond in more positive ways than they normally would under non-test settings. Similarly, researchers *want* the project to succeed, so they might perceive, code, and analyze data more positively. These limitations are known in social science research as reactivity, and they underscore some of the major differences between traditional and community-based research. Activist researchers should be aware of these risks and be prepared to respond to IRBs and peer reviewers who want to know how the risks will be addressed.

Lastly, of course, was the limitation of the power dynamic that overshadowed the entire CWEST project. While Allen and Jaclyn tried to work in an equal and reciprocal manner, they were still PhD students from across the river. Moreover, they were developing literacy resources for the Purdue OWL, which millions of users accessed every year. LARA teachers and WorkOne volunteers had used the OWL for years themselves, so the authors could not fully escape the power dynamic despite their best efforts at designing a collaborative project using reciprocal research methods.

Nonetheless, the authors used best practices to try to minimize all of these risks. Their efforts included telling participants that they were genuinely interested in their views and responses and that they were using empirical methods to tailor the resources to their needs. Jaclyn and Allen also pointed out that the participants were not being tested on their ability to use technology, but rather that the *resources* were being tested for their effectiveness. The authors also reminded participants that they could stop testing any time.

The authors tried to minimize Halo and Expectancy Effects by reiterating the need for candid feedback on the project and its deliverables. Moreover, since Jaclyn and Allen worked together, they were able to challenge each other's assumptions and findings. One result of this critical research process, informed by Sullivan and Porter's (1997) *Opening Spaces*, is realizing that while the project succeeded on many levels, it did not fulfill its objective of widespread use throughout LARA/WorkOne.

As noted above, at the completion of the study many teachers, volunteers, and end users were still not using the online resources. Some LARA/WorkOne users integrated the resources into their teaching and learning, but the technology barrier, despite usability testing, still seemed difficult to overcome for many people. For them, printing the digital resources worked best. Nowhere was this more obvious than when Allen volunteered as a LARA tutor a few months before the CWEST research concluded.

Tutoring at LARA

A few months before research at LARA/WorkOne concluded, Allen completed summer tutor training and volunteered at LARA. By this point, he was heavily invested in the LARA/WorkOne mission and simply wanted to make a positive difference beyond what the authors had accomplished with the CWEST. Once per week, usually on Fridays, he would tutor LARA learners as they prepared to take the GED. At the same time, a licensed teacher worked with the high-school students who were attending LARA to receive credits and complete their diplomas.

During this time, Allen tutored a wide range of learners from various backgrounds. And like his first days at LARA as a researcher, Allen was reminded of his experiences in the three writing centers he had worked in, as well as his time at Bryant Adult Education Center. The LARA teachers even asked Allen to share his story with the students. The administrators thought that hearing this experience would help people realize that adult education could help them do something positive with their lives.

Allen recalls one LARA learner in particular, Lawrence, who was struggling with all of his subjects but especially with the LARA atmosphere and interaction with other troubled students. Lawrence was African-American, came from a single-parent household, and he had dropped out of high school. His mother worked two jobs while he went to LARA to finish his diploma.

Lawrence told Allen one Friday that his only hope of making any real money for his family was through mixed martial arts (MMA). He had trained extensively and was in incredible physical shape, but he also found it difficult to control his temper.

"That's why I got kicked out of high school," he said. "This guy disrespected me, and we got into a fight. He lost. I mean, that's what I do to make money, you know? I fight. So yeah, he lost, and I got kicked out."

Lawrence reminded Allen of himself in high school, though their racial and socioeconomic situations differed greatly. The two talked more about staying at LARA to complete a diploma, and Lawrence said it was difficult because he could have been working a job during the day and fighting at night to make ends meet. After that first talk, Allen didn't see Lawrence for a couple of weeks. He heard from a LARA teacher that Lawrence had gotten into a shoving match with another guy, who was also struggling with finishing his high-school credits.

When Allen saw Lawrence again, he told his story about Hayfield and Robert E. Lee high schools and about Bryant. They ended up talking for quite a while.

"Wow. You got kicked out of *two* high schools?" Lawrence asked. "That's more than me. If I get kicked out of LARA, it will be a draw!" Lawrence pointed out.

"This isn't a match you want to win, Lawrence," Allen replied, and encouraged him to finish his diploma at LARA.

Then Lawrence told Allen about the shoving match he had gotten into and got really upset as he explained what happened.

"That guy insulted me. I'm gonna' crush him like I crushed that punk at my high school," Lawrence said.

Remembering his time playing baseball and football, and his associated injuries, Allen replied "Lawrence, if you actually get into a fight, they're going to kick you out for good, and then all you'll have is fighting. And how long can that last? With one kick to your knee, your career could be over. You'll be an ex-amateur MMA fighter with a bum knee."

Allen's comments seemed to sink in, but unfortunately, that was the last time Allen saw Lawrence, and the authors never found out if he ever finished his diploma at LARA. Like the Bryant administrator who took Allen into an office and talked some sense into him, Allen wanted to help Lawrence make some positive changes in his life. Of course it was easier for Allen to stay at

Bryant because he had a more stable home life and more options because of his socioeconomic situation. Nevertheless, Allen hoped that in some way he had helped Lawrence make the right choice by staying at LARA.

In the larger picture, both Jaclyn and Allen believe that they sustained a small victory by collaborating with LARA/WorkOne as much as they could, and by completing their work as carefully and thoroughly as they could, informed by theory and experience, and aided by empirical research. Admittedly, however, the authors have often wondered about the level of success they achieved with the CWEST based on their mixed results. Personally, Allen wonders the same when reflecting on his interaction with Lawrence.

When Allen returned to the classroom after his interaction with Lawrence, the LARA teacher asked him to work with a student who was preparing for the writing section of the GED test. Allen was excited because the teacher said that the student was curious about the CWEST resources. The student and Allen worked with the materials, and he seemed to like them. He liked that he could access the resources online at the library, where he usually got on to the Internet. During this tutoring shift, another LARA teacher was working with a student using the CWEST resources printed out in a binder.

This experience illustrated that even though the CWEST resources had not been adopted by a large number of teachers or students, some teachers and learners *did* use them. Still, Allen confirmed firsthand during his tutoring experience what the initial research findings had indicated: Only a fraction of LARA teachers used the CWEST. Sam, the WorkOne coordinator, used the WorkOne materials, but the volunteers he worked with used them only occasionally. Sam retired shortly after the CWEST project concluded, which may have meant that even fewer WorkOne folks used the materials.

Both of these examples illustrate why fostering long-term relationships and collecting longitudinal data is so important for these types of community-based research projects. These examples also show why it is important for faculty members and writing centers to maintain programs like the CWEST—faculty members can be long-term fixtures at universities in a way that students cannot, and writing centers can work as stable places for sustained civic engagement.

Though the CWEST project was fairly well funded and took place over three years, the authors still had a finite amount of time to work, and only two people were on the project; moreover, their time was split among various graduate student responsibilities. Therefore, the iterative design process was limited to three stages and two generations of usability testing.

The authors might have conducted a final round of tests to measure the revisions made after the second round of testing and continued to collect longitudinal data on CWEST use. Also, with more time and resources, the authors might have been able to recruit more WorkOne participants to submit documents to more human resource raters who in turn might have provided more diverse feedback on participants' job documents.

While the independent raters Allen recruited represented the WorkOne participants' audience, it is risky to overgeneralize the writing assessment findings. To conclude that a large number of human resource experts would rate the revised documents as effective or improved is making an unsubstantiated claim. Lastly, since the authors were unable to stay in contact with the WorkOne participants who used the online resources to revise their job search documents, they could not determine whether or not these participants ultimately obtained jobs.

Final Reflections on the CWEST

While the authors are reluctant to proclaim complete success, findings from the interviews, observations, focus groups, the two generations of usability testing, and the writing assessment indicated that the methodology used for the project helped them develop and implement the CWEST in a collaborative way while also systematically recording feedback. Findings also suggested that the community participants considered the model helpful in building a close collaboration between the Purdue Writing Lab and LARA/WorkOne.

Some LARA instructors and learners used the GED and ESL resources to help them progress through their educational goals. Some WorkOne volunteers and clients used the job search resources to further their employment goals. Moreover, findings indicated that the research methods helped improve the project as the authors developed and improved the deliverables they produced with community partners. Lastly, findings suggested that the job search document resources helped participants write more effective résumés and cover letters and helped participants improve their professional ethos.

As noted above, however, despite the theory, empirical methods, and care given in running this project, the authors did not fulfill all of the project goals, one of which was widespread adoption of the online CWEST resources at LARA/WorkOne. Participants who already felt comfortable with technology found the online resources helpful and were enthusiastic about the material and the project, but only a few of the "technologically nervous" participants adopted the online resources. A fair number of LARA/WorkOne teachers and volunteers printed out the material.

Though global online use of the CWEST materials through the Purdue OWL is encouraging, Jaclyn and Allen still hesitate to proclaim this project a success. However, they hope that readers who are learning about the messiness of community work do not shy away from civic engagement. Rather, they hope that this book helps foster *careful* and long-term civic engagement.

As the authors have asserted throughout this book, they strongly encourage using a model that is informed by scholarship and theory, that is guided by empirical research of some form, and that helps stakeholders develop strong personal connections. Allen and Jaclyn believe that when activist researchers and writing center administrators use this approach, they can avoid some of the stumbles outlined here and perhaps even build on some of the CWEST project's successes.

KEY TAKEAWAYS

Though the CWEST project enjoyed many successes, the authors learned the greatest lessons from the project's many challenges, limitations, and even outright failures. These lessons may be useful for others hoping to do local work in their communities and writing centers. A few of Jaclyn and Allen's most important lessons include the following:

- **Community-based research is "real" and action oriented.** We often think of research as something that happens behind closed doors or that is removed from real experience. Community-based research happens on the ground, in the thick of engagement, and it solves (or tries to solve) real problems in our communities.
- **Community-based research works more effectively when it integrates a participatory, iterative, and empirical process.** Working collaboratively and reciprocally, college and community partners can develop, test, revise, and maintain effective processes and products that benefit all stakeholders.
- **Community-based research can benefit from technology, but activist-researchers must exercise great care (see above) in using it.** The digital divide most acutely felt by marginalized populations must be closed and not widened by college-community collaboration.
- **Community-based research generally works best if it is long term.** Though short-term projects can have value, long-term commitment and personal relationships between stakeholders generally produce more positive outcomes.
- **Community researchers are engaged participants.** While "The Researcher" is sometimes cast as an objective and distanced presence, in community-based research, the boundary between researcher and participant is blurred. Community researchers should embrace their participant role, as doing so can create more productive, engaged research.

- **Community-based research requires flexibility.** In community-based research, the path from raising questions to analyzing findings is anything but neat and linear. Researchers should embrace this messiness and stay open to raising new questions and reshaping their approach and methods.
- **Community-based research comes with potential challenges**, including participant recruitment and retention, troubling power dynamics between community and college members, and biases that can influence findings about the engagement project being studied. Researchers should be aware of these challenges and think about how they will manage them.
- **College and community teaching contexts may differ greatly.** For example, a university writing center and a community literacy center may use markedly different teaching strategies. College and community educators should not only stay attuned to moments of shared understanding but also know that their experiences may not translate perfectly to the different context.

Nevertheless . . .

- **Community-based research can and should be explored and implemented by writing centers**. Though civic work can be challenging when developed and maintained by writing center faculty, staff, and tutors, writing centers can be stable platforms for community engagement. They have a natural overlap with community literacy efforts that span age groups, races, and socioeconomic and cultural contexts.

Chapter 6

Engagement as Professional Work

This chapter focuses on the authors' current work as faculty members. The authors hope to provide a model for learning from community-based work, as well as further the conversation about how community engagement both parallels and informs more traditional areas of faculty responsibilities. Figure 6.1 presents the continuing steps the authors are taking as they apply what they learned during the CWEST to their current community work. Two steps have been added to this emergent methodology: reflect on project and apply lessons learned; if possible, continue working with community.

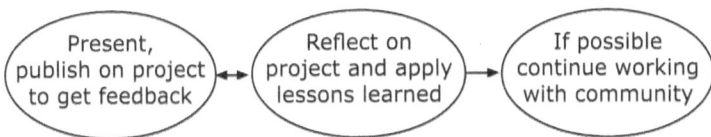

Figure 6.1 Steps for Moving Forward

This chapter argues that faculty members can draw from their expertise as teachers, researchers, and administrators in developing community engagement projects, and that community-based work can inform teaching, research, and administration. The authors show how faculty members might accomplish these diverse tasks by using the engaged scholarship model posited by Ernest L. Boyer (1990). Boyer's model envisions faculty work—teaching, research, service—as overlapping and informing one another. To illustrate this approach, the authors discuss their civic engagement as faculty members.

ENGAGED SCHOLARSHIP: HOW THE CWEST INFORMS ALLEN'S COMMUNITY-BASED WORK IN BALTIMORE

As many readers of this book may already know, the transition from graduate student to faculty member can be chaotic and a bit terrifying. Despite years of professionalization, which usually includes teaching, research, and service responsibilities, new-hire faculty members can become overwhelmed by their full-time positions. After beginning his first faculty position, Allen quickly realized that if he wished to continue his community-focused work, he would have to find a way to *center* his diverse responsibilities on engagement.

Thankfully, Allen experienced excellent preparation at his graduate institution and outstanding mentorship at his faculty institution; both allowed him to develop the engaged approach he desired in his new position. In one particularly influential example, the director of service-learning at his new institution, Robin Crews, introduced Allen to the work of Ernest L. Boyer (1990), who posited a civic approach to scholarship that helps faculty members fulfill tenure-track responsibilities; Boyer called this approach the scholarship of application, which has since been called engaged scholarship.

Allen was hired at Loyola University Maryland in 2010 as a tenure-track assistant professor of writing in the writing department. At the time of printing, it has been five years since the authors collaborated on the CWEST, but Allen's experience in the project prepared him for many of the responsibilities of this position at Loyola. These responsibilities include teaching a variety of writing courses in a 3-3 load: professional writing, writing for the Web, introduction to rhetoric, and the department's core first-year composition (FYC) course, effective writing.

Additionally, Allen works as the department's internship coordinator, teaches internship courses, and serves on department and university committees. Lastly, he assists students as a core and major advisor. He was hired to invigorate professional writing in the department and to support Loyola's Jesuit mission of social justice. As such, Allen is well positioned to center his work—teaching, research, and service—on community engagement. Since Allen was not hired to work in Loyola's writing center, he had to figure out how to enter into civic engagement through course-based pedagogy.

Through Boyer's (1990) model of engaged scholarship, Allen aligns his efforts with institutional goals—a lesson learned from Linda Bergmann. He follows this approach as a next step to civic work that moves beyond the traditional models of extension, outreach, and one-way service-learning. Of all his faculty responsibilities, Allen asks himself: "How can this project or responsibility interact with or inform my community work?" In this way, he is also able to accomplish community-centered work while fulfilling teaching, research, and service. Figure 6.2 illustrates this model.

Like many civic engagement projects, Allen's latest effort has involved a mixture of intense research, anxious meetings with community partners,

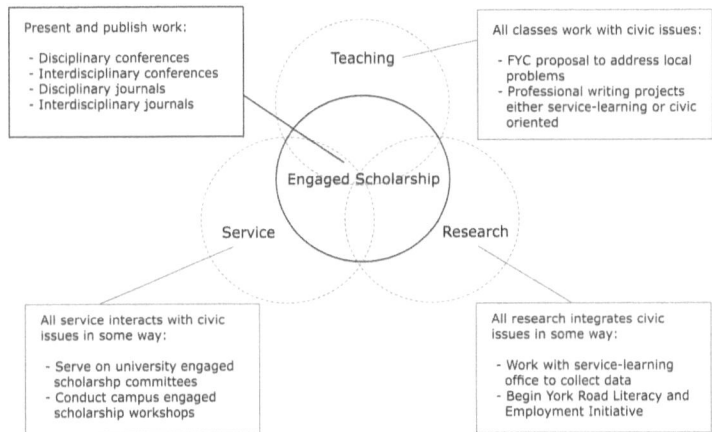

Figure 6.2 Allen's Engaged Scholarship at Loyola

nervous students, and mixed success. But the project also experienced some great accomplishments. Guided by his experience with the CWEST, as well as the engaged scholarship model, Allen has learned to organize his time and take most of these ups and downs in stride.

Scholars have long discussed challenges to community-oriented work, only one of which is the fact that semester schedules differ greatly from the schedules of nonprofits and foundations. Other issues include logistical challenges of getting students from campus to service sites, as well as inconsistent support and funding. Maintaining long-term relationships with community partners has helped Allen overcome these challenges; if things temporarily fall apart, he and his partners can reorganize the service-learning project and continue work the following term.

Despite sustained relationships with community partners and extensive research accompanied by long discussions with local activists, Allen is surprised by some of the experiences he and his students in Baltimore have had. Issues of socioeconomic class, race, and religion change so that what works one semester doesn't work the next. This is one reason he has remained flexible and drawn on the lessons he and Jaclyn learned from the CWEST project, as well as literature from engaged scholarship.

The York Road Literacy and Employment Initiative

The York Road Literacy and Employment Initiative (YRLEI) is designed to build on the CWEST project; like the CWEST, the YRLEI focuses on literacy and employment issues. Allen has also replicated some of the methods used for the CWEST. The YRLEI project seeks to help improve writing and technology literacies among Baltimore community members.

Covering literacy and employment, the YRLEI project seeks to assist Baltimore community members in finding and obtaining jobs. This is an especially important direction for community work in Baltimore because local researchers and activists are finding that people in challenged socioeconomic situations are not able to rebound from the recession as easily as those in the middle class. Nowhere is this clearer than in the neighborhoods located near Loyola's campus.

Loyola straddles the line between historically white, wealthy neighborhoods like Roland Park and Homeland, and traditionally African-American neighborhoods, like Richnor Springs and greater Govans, that were hit hard by the recession and have long been suffering from the effects of redlining[1] and blockbusting.[2] Located near Loyola's campus, Govans is home to many socioeconomically challenged residents. Loyola, therefore, rests between what is known as a "rich" street, North Charles, and what is known locally as a "poor" street, York Road.

To help address this socioeconomic dichotomy, Loyola began focusing on social justice and community issues along the York Road Corridor as a part of its Jesuit and Catholic mission. The university launched the "Loyola is Listening" campaign in 2010, coincidentally the year Allen was hired. Loyola conducted the listening project to determine the specific concerns of residents along the York Road Corridor.

Participants in the Loyola is Listening project identified a number of needs, which included the area's digital divide and unemployment. In response to these needs, and guided by the CWEST project, Allen designed the YRLEI as a technologically driven literacy and jobs project that also aligned with Loyola's mission. To enact the YRLEI, he followed a reciprocal, sustainable, and iterative process, which integrated participatory and empirical methods similar to the CWEST project.

Though Allen didn't have a clear idea of how the YRLEI would mature when he began service-learning classes in spring 2011, he knew that he wanted to do something with local communities. Since his part of the CWEST project did not include participation from writing students at Purdue, he was also interested in integrating his current work in civic engagement with his pedagogy at Loyola. As noted previously, Allen also had to integrate civic work into course-based pedagogy instead of the writing center, since his position did not include a writing center role.

Guided by Bowden and Scott's (2004) book, *Service-Learning in Technical and Professional Communication* as well as his experiences with the CWEST, Allen designed a project that combined teaching, research, and service over a long period of time. Of particular interest to Allen from

Bowden and Scott's (2004) text was the process of cooperation they suggest for students and community partners to collaborate on deliverables. As a result, YRLEI now includes a number of partners, some of whom are described here:

- *Loyola University Maryland*: Located in north Baltimore, Loyola is a Jesuit, Catholic comprehensive university that maintains a strong tradition of social justice and civic engagement. Loyola is designated as a Community Engagement campus by the Carnegie Foundation for the Advancement of Teaching.
- *Richnor Springs Neighborhood Association* (RSNA): The RSNA is one of many community organizations that form the York Road Corridor; RSNA is the first community group Allen worked with in spring 2011.
- *Govans Ecumenical Development Corporation* (GEDCO)/CARES: GEDCO/CARES is a large conglomeration of nonprofit, secular, and faith-based organizations serving Govans-area citizens in a variety of ways: housing, rent support, food, education, and employment; Allen began working with them in spring 2014 to organize the literacy workshops.

Allen and his students have collaborated with these partners through multiple semesters of work and have produced scores of deliverables. The students have also conducted many hours of interviews, completed neighborhood clean ups, and co-created community websites. Guiding all of these efforts are the major conclusions Allen and Jaclyn developed from the CWEST: YRLEI is theory informed, empirically driven, iterative, sustained, and reciprocal. Moreover, Allen and his students have formed strong personal relationships with all of their community partners.

The YRLEI has become a multiyear, IRB-approved community-based research project. To achieve this, the project was organized into four phases:

1. Service-learning with Richnor Springs, a socioeconomically challenged neighborhood in the Govans area near Loyola
2. Literacy resource development with Richnor Springs
3. Literacy resource online posting and testing with GEDCO/CARES
4. Literacy and employment workshops with GEDCO/CARES

In keeping with the empirical methods of the CWEST, Allen (with help from Loyola's office of service-learning) collected qualitative and quantitative data during every step of this project. Though the first four phases of work are now complete, Allen and his students are continuing work with RSNA and GEDCO/CARES. The following few paragraphs provide an overall timeline of the YRLEI project.

The project began in *spring 2011*, when service-learning students from Allen's Art of Rhetoric class conducted secondary research and interviewed Richnor Springs residents to learn more about the neighborhood. During this semester, students also produced an information report and an environmentally friendly, laminated neighborhood association meeting sign.

The project continued in *fall 2011*. During this semester, service-learning students from Allen's Rhetoric of Professional Writing class collaborated with RSNA to produce their first self-designed association website. RSNA had a website already, but it was set up and run by an organization with what Allen argues are for-profit interests (LiveBaltimore), though it claims otherwise.

In *spring 2012*, service-learning students from Allen's Technical Writing class conducted usability testing with their peers (a non-IRB-approved class project) to collect data on the new RSNA website, and they composed a report suggesting changes. At this point, Allen began working with Loyola's IRB to prepare for qualitative and quantitative data collection involving students and community partners. He also began working with Loyola's Office of Research and Sponsored Programs to obtain funding.

In *fall 2013*, the work continued in Allen's Writing for the Web class. During this semester, service-learning students collaborated with RSNA to redesign their neighborhood website using WordPress, so community members could work on the site themselves. Students also participated in a vacant lot cleanup in Richnor Springs; this work clearly differed from the students' usual professional and technical writing projects but is still significant, as it shows their growing investment in the area.

In *spring 2014*, service-learning students from Allen's Rhetoric of Professional Writing class collaborated with RSNA to develop literacy resources inspired by the CWEST project. This was the beginning of the IRB-approved interview research with Allen's service-learning students and Richnor Springs community participants. Like the fall 2013 students, students in this course also participated in an adopted lot and neighborhood cleanup project.

During spring 2014, Allen also learned that the community-based research project was awarded an undergraduate research assistant grant (the Kolvenbach Summer Research Award) and a faculty summer research grant. The Kolvenbach awarded a stipend of $3,500 for a research assistant with an additional $500 going to the community partner and $500 for Allen's research needs. The summer research grant provided $4,000 to help reimburse participants with $50 gift cards and food.

In keeping with the transparent approach to describing the CWEST project, the following lists detail the total YRLEI project budget:

Literacy resource development, testing, and workshop attendee reimbursement

- Community partner interviews (4 people @ $50): $200
- Testing session on website and literacy resources (11 people @ $50): $550
- Three workshops (20 people @ $50 * 3 workshops): $3,000
- Document evaluators for pre- and post-workshop cover letter and résumé drafts (2 human resource experts @ $50 each): $100

Transcription

- Interviews (10 hours total): $450

Food

- Test session snacks: $20
- Workshop lunches (20 * $3 * 3 workshops): $180

Workshop attendee flash drives (paid for with separate funding from CCSJ)

- 50 4GB flip flash drives: $50

Total budget: $4,550

Allen and his undergraduate research assistant, Giuliana Caranante (now a graduate student in Clemson's master of arts in professional communication), were able to garner considerable institutional support. In part, Allen and Giuliana may have been successful at gaining support because they aligned the work so closely with Loyola's Jesuit mission and its focus on local social justice issues. Toward the middle of summer 2014, Giuliana and Allen posted the completed literacy resources to the Web and conducted usability tests with GEDCO/CARES clients to get feedback.

Later that summer, Giuliana and Allen revised the online literacy resources and used them for three community literacy workshops in conjunction with GEDCO/CARES:

- Workshop 1: Using the Internet and MS Word
- Workshop 2: Writing Effective Cover Letters and Résumés
- Workshop 3: Preparing for Job Interviews

Allen and Giuliana collected qualitative and quantitative data from workshop attendees to inform future revision of the resources and workshops.

This brings us to fall 2014, when Allen took a pre-tenure research leave to code and analyze all of this data. To code and analyze data, Giuliana and Allen used descriptive statistics and grounded theory with NVivo (a qualitative data program), and they began work on the two articles emerging from this project; they are collaborating with a quantitative specialist in the communication department at Loyola, Paola Pascual-Ferrá. This approach highlights the interdisciplinary possibilities of these types of community-based research projects.

In spring 2015, Allen and Giuliana followed up with the service-learning students and community members from the spring 2014 service-learning project to collect some longitudinal data. Lastly, GEDCO/CARES helped Allen and Giuliana track data for their clients who got interviews and jobs after they attended the workshops; GEDCO/CARES collects this data at the one-month, three-month, and six-month points.

Addressing Shortcomings from the CWEST

Though the CWEST enjoyed many successes, some of the authors' most important findings had to do with the project's shortcomings. As discussed in the previous chapter, these shortcomings included an inaccurate idea of the community partner's skills in literacy and technology; mixed results regarding participant recruitment and retention; lack of widespread adoption of literacy resources; and lack of longitudinal data to track outcomes of project.

In designing the YRLEI, Allen drew on conversations with Jaclyn about shortcomings of the CWEST. He also received valuable feedback from anonymous journal and conference reviewers, as well as journal editors. To address the CWEST's shortcomings (particularly, the four major shortcomings listed in the previous paragraph), and to integrate Boyer's (1990) engaged scholarship model, Allen used some different strategies for the YRLEI.

Addressing Inaccurate Idea of Community Partner Skills in Literacy and Technology

To address the inaccurate idea of community partner skills in literacy and technology from the CWEST, Allen relied on the "Loyola is Listening" data, data from other local studies, his ongoing work with Richnor Springs, and his interview data from spring 2014. The "Loyola is Listening" project found that literacy and the digital divide are pressing problems in the North Baltimore Govans area. When Allen began interviewing community members in spring 2014, he focused some questions on literacy and technology. Initial findings confirm larger studies conducted in Baltimore.

These conclusions provided a detailed view of larger findings from other studies on poverty, literacy, and employment in Baltimore. Although the city has addressed issues of literacy and college/career readiness in the past decade, many of these achievements have been blunted by the crippling effects of the recession and the subprime mortgage crisis. Illiteracy, which impacts education and employment, remains high: "In 2009, roughly 99,000 Baltimore City adults did not have a high school diploma."[3] Baltimore's unemployment rate also remains high at 10.3 percent.[4]

This empirical data was reinforced by experiential information gleaned from Allen's ongoing work with Richnor Springs. Literacy, technology, and employment were pressing issues for the people living just across the street from some of the wealthiest, well-educated neighborhoods in Baltimore, further evidence of racist redlining and blockbusting in the Charm City. Through his interaction with community members, Allen learned that the literacy skills of job-seeking residents were especially challenged. These challenges intensified in older and retired people, particularly in areas of technology.

Based on this primary and secondary research, as well as his experiential knowledge, Allen felt that he had a better idea of his community partners' literacy and technology skills than when he and Jaclyn began the CWEST. A more accurate notion of the community partners' literacy and technology skills also helped Giuliana and Allen revise the YRLEI online resources as they moved into the workshop phase of the project.

The workshops themselves were another important addition driven by the shortcomings of the CWEST project. Jaclyn and Allen worked with community partners to develop and launch CWEST resources, but they worked with them to *use* the material only here and there (during Allen's tutoring experience with LARA and Jaclyn's impromptu tutorials during LARA observations). Therefore, it was important that Giuliana and Allen work with both GEDCO/CARES teachers and end users to help them understand how the resources can work for individuals and in workshop settings.

Addressing Mixed Results Regarding Participant Recruitment and Retention

To address mixed results regarding participant recruitment and retention, Allen drew upon his long-term collaboration with Richnor Springs. The community members Allen worked with knew him and his students, and the local residents were committed to helping develop effective, tailored, and usable resources. In addition, Allen was very careful when choosing a nonprofit organization—GEDCO/CARES—to help him and Giuliana with the workshops.

GEDCO/CARES was also central to addressing participant recruitment and retention problems. GEDCO/CARES not only shares a similar mission of focusing on literacy and employment, but it also has a solid track record of working with Loyola and with the local community. In fact, people who serve on the GEDCO/CARES board of directors work closely with Loyola. When Allen approached GEDCO/CARES about collaborating with them on research and workshops, they responded enthusiastically and even helped to recruit participants.

Allen also adjusted the amount and the distribution strategy of participant reimbursement. Participants received a $50 gift card for the feedback/usability session. They also received a $50 gift card for each workshop they attended, as well as a lunch and a flash drive to store their work.[5] Unlike his experience with the CWEST, Allen was able to recruit and retain enough participants to collect sufficient data for all stages of the study.

Addressing Lack of Widespread Adoption

To address the lack of widespread adoption of resources by community partners, Allen integrated four additions into the YRLEI. First, Giuliana and Allen conducted usability tests to raise awareness among end users and GEDCO/CARES staff. Second, they ran literacy workshops to collaborate closely with community partners in *using* the resources. Third, they provided free flash drives to help attendees save resources and their work. Fourth, they will be posting final drafts on the GEDCO/CARES website.

Conducting the CWEST usability tests helped Jaclyn and Allen obtain feedback from the community partners, which was not a surprising outcome. However, they were surprised that these test sessions also worked as training sessions on the resources, and they raised awareness of the project among LARA/WorkOne staff and students. So Allen knew that beyond getting valuable feedback from current participants, usability sessions would help the community partners at GEDCO/CARES gain experience on the resources and spread the word about the work. This word of mouth led to full workshops.

The workshops also succeeded in building a face-to-face relationship with community partners over time. Allen used his experience as the Purdue OWL coordinator, Writing Lab tutor, and writing instructor to help design workshops that were part lecture, part group work, and part writing activities. Based on his experience with Jaclyn and Sam at the Sunrise Diner, he made sure that he and Giuliana provided lunch so partners could all "break bread" together.

Based on observations at WorkOne, Allen remembered that one of the main problems clients had was remembering important employment information. (For an example, see chapter 4's discussion of Amanda.) Moreover, many WorkOne clients had to save their résumés on WorkOne computers because they did not have PCs at home, and they did not own CDs or computer disks. To increase widespread adoption of the YRLEI resources and help people save their work and keep it with them, Allen distributed flash drives that included the literacy material during workshops.

Addressing Lack of Longitudinal Data to Track Outcomes

To address the lack of longitudinal data to track project outcomes for the CWEST, Allen asked his GEDCO/CARES partners how he might record employment information for workshop attendees. He was very happy to learn that they were willing to help track this data using two databases they maintain for their clients and for funding. Together, therefore, Allen and the community partner tracked workshop attendees' job interviews (whether or not they have them, and if so, how many), whether or not they obtained jobs, and how long they remained at those jobs.

Allen and GEDCO/CARES staff also tracked job benefits, such as healthcare and retirement. They began looking at this data at the one-month mark after the workshops. They are currently coding and analyzing this data to assess and improve the project itself and to collect information for future publications. At this point, however, Allen *can* report that most participants responded positively to the project and that seven of the fourteen workshop participants obtained jobs.

Integrating an engaged scholarship approach into his professional work has allowed Allen to connect community-based work to most of his responsibilities as a tenure-track faculty member. Moreover, the YRLEI stakeholders in Baltimore would not have achieved so much without the experiences he and Jaclyn shared with their community partners on the CWEST in Lafayette, Indiana.

The long road and the challenges that faced Allen and Jaclyn in the CWEST project could have prevented them from taking those first steps in collaborating with LARA and WorkOne. But after looking back at their work together and after working on his current civic engagement project, Allen feels comfortable saying that once activist-scholars have prepared themselves as best they can, they just have to take those first difficult steps.

DIVERSE ROLES AND RESPONSIBILITIES: HOW THE CWEST INFORMS JACLYN'S WRITING CENTER WORK

Several years have passed since the authors began the CWEST project. At the time of this writing, Jaclyn is in a faculty position at the University of Alabama at Birmingham (UAB), an urban public research university. In this position, she is a tenure-track faculty member in the English department and director of the university writing center. This position requires Jaclyn to balance an assortment of responsibilities and negotiate diverse, sometimes conflicting, roles.

These responsibilities include a heavy administrative load, in addition to usual faculty responsibilities of teaching, scholarship, and service. Further, much of Jaclyn's teaching and scholarship engages the community, so in both, she adds "community participant" to her roles. For Jaclyn, the CWEST project provided experience balancing diverse roles and responsibilities, negotiating competing demands, and creating meaningful connections among different areas of work.

During the CWEST project, Jaclyn's thinking about community engagement often resembled her thinking about writing program administration,[6] which she was studying as her secondary area at Purdue. In many ways, perceptions of community-based work parallel those of writing program administration. Where community-based work is often regarded as extra rather than central, writing program administration is very often regarded as necessary but merely managerial, the work that must be done to keep the trains running but that lies outside of the "real" work of research and teaching.

In both the cases, the work may also be viewed as mere service. In *GenAdmin: Theorizing WPA Identities in the Twenty-First Century*, Charlton et al. (2011) wrote from the perspectives of writing program administrators who have chosen and prepared for WPA work and who see such work as central to their professional identities. Throughout *GenAdmin*, the authors reflect on the need to reposition writing program administration as scholarly, meaningful work that some faculty seek out, as opposed to managerial or service work that some unfortunate faculty get saddled with or take their turn at.

Those who choose community engagement and community-based research face similar complications in staking out a professional identity, as the work may be seen as an add-on or mere service in ways that are similar to administration. For Jaclyn, both writing program administration and community engagement became significant professional interests, central to her work as a scholar and teacher rather than something to do in her spare time away from teaching and researching.[7]

The previous section describes how the Boyer (1990) model has helped Allen to re-envision the traditional approach to scholarship and ultimately allowed him to shape his faculty work in ways that more realistically reflect the kind of thinker, teacher, and activist he wishes to be. The Boyer model allows for the addition of a community-focused agenda precisely because that agenda is not *additional*.

Rather, a community-focused orientation can run through the three traditional "legs" of faculty work (service, scholarship, and teaching). The Boyer model may also provide WPAs like Jaclyn useful ways of rethinking their work, as elevating the application of disciplinary expertise clearly supports the idea of administrative work as scholarly. This section describes this and other connections between administrative and community-based work and argues that Jaclyn's experiences in the CWEST prepared her in important ways for her faculty position and its administrative responsibilities.

"But Is It Working?": Assessing the Program You Love

Jaclyn's work as a writing center director perhaps best illustrates how the CWEST prepared her to balance diverse roles and negotiate competing demands. Often, her greatest challenges include assessing, researching, and revising the center and communicating about its successes and challenges with diverse stakeholders. These types of work also formed central parts of the CWEST project. Additionally, in both community and writing center contexts, assessment, research, and communication are occasionally challenged, at least emotionally, by leaders' dedication to the programs.

Like the authors in *GenAdmin*, Jaclyn prepared for and sought out an administrative position, and she views writing program administration as central to her professional identity. Specifically, she wanted to direct a writing center because she felt strongly that one-on-one teaching provides an invaluable opportunity for students at all levels and in all areas of study to improve as writers. Directing such a program, Jaclyn believed, would prove tremendously gratifying.

Jaclyn's interest in writing centers began while she tutored during her MA program and then increased at Purdue, where she developed a close relationship with Linda Bergmann, director of the Writing Lab. She and Allen witnessed daily the humor and life that Linda brought to the job, and they watched her function as the ringleader of a program that served as a hub for writing on the university's enormous campus (and, through the Purdue OWL, as a resource for writers all over the world). Jaclyn wanted such a position.

Jaclyn's favorite part of directing the writing center is observing and soaking up the energy that comes from the collaboration and relationships unfolding there daily. Just like Purdue's Writing Lab, UAB's writing center affords constant opportunities to talk with students and faculty from all over campus. In a word, the work is *fun*. Lynn Z. Bloom (2002) shares the following quote from a survey respondent at the beginning of "Are We Having Fun Yet? Necessity, Creativity, and Writing Program Administration": "Simply put, everything I do as a WPA is fun. If it wasn't, I wouldn't do it" (p. 57).

At the same time, Doug Hesse (1999) argues in "The WPA as Father, Husband, Ex" that administrators can risk overattachment to the programs they direct. Overattachment can result in exhausted administrators who feel so strongly about their programs that honest assessment of them becomes difficult. For Jaclyn, the center feels like home. She finds herself referring in daily conversation to it as "her" writing center, possessive language that may even slip into the present chapter. Like many directors who truly love the work, Jaclyn certainly experiences moments of caring perhaps too much.

Readers may debate the healthiness of Jaclyn's attachment to "her" writing center, but eliminating that attachment might matter less than working productively within it. This means channeling dedication for the center productively by assessing and improving its work, instead of destructively, by reacting defensively to criticism. In addition to providing experience with assessment methods, then, the CWEST project prepared Jaclyn for negotiating her commitment to a program with the need to assess it realistically.

Jaclyn's earliest assessments of the writing center help illustrate both the methods and the thick skin necessary to honestly answering questions about how the center was working. When she began the position at UAB, most of its writing center's clients came from English courses, and particularly from the developmental English course that required writing center use. Jaclyn's early assessments of the writing center reflected her initial goal: to increase usage, particularly among students outside of English classes.

This type of assessment was relatively easy to conduct but admittedly difficult for Jaclyn's psyche. In the clearest sense, she was questioning if her efforts to promote and expand the writing center were working. She had asked for more funding, hired new tutors, and widely advertised services, but what was the result? To address that question, Jaclyn did quantitative assessments that will look familiar to most writing center directors and tutors. Her writing center now does this type of "bean-counting," to borrow from Lerner (1997), every semester, along with voluntary student evaluations after sessions.

These assessments have suggested many positives. The center's usage has increased steadily and students overwhelmingly respond with high evaluations. Still, the assessment has uncovered issues. For example, the center sees many more first-year and second-year students than upper-level undergraduates, which suggests that its services may prove less valuable (or are at least perceived as less valuable) to students in upper-level and/or major courses. Jaclyn's experience with the CWEST project prepared her to see these kinds of nuances in assessment results and to resist success narratives.

The CWEST project also provided experience in seeking the full picture of a program by studying it from a variety of angles, or in other words, using a variety of assessment methods. Allen and Jaclyn investigated the CWEST through an assortment of qualitative and quantitative methods, including interviews with teachers and students, observations, usability testing, and collection of artifacts. Jaclyn also looks at the writing center through multiple lenses.

In addition to collecting data about usage and clients and gathering student (and sometimes faculty) surveys, Jaclyn runs each semester a different kind of focused assessment. Following the advice of Schendel and Macauley (2012) in *Building Writing Center Assessments That Matter*, Jaclyn recognizes that she cannot assess every aspect of the writing center all of the time. She can, however, raise questions and address them using more focused assessments that supplement the center's continual data collection about tutoring sessions, clients, and student and faculty response.

Action-Oriented, Applicable Research

Developing, researching, and revising the CWEST project also equipped Jaclyn with an action-focused orientation toward research that in some ways has muddied her distinction between writing center research and assessment. While research and assessment differ, Jaclyn's approach to research means using findings to immediately and directly inform the writing center in a way that is often reserved for information gathered from local assessments.

As the authors have tried to illustrate throughout the book, applying research findings directly and immediately to improving the CWEST project itself was always a central goal. In the writing center, Jaclyn follows this model precisely. When she conducts research and assessments about the writing center, she always hopes to find information that will directly impact its work. Following the Boyer model, this orientation toward research elevates the application of new knowledge and opens the possibility for a more integrated approach to faculty work.

In one example, Jaclyn recently conducted a mixed-methods study on student perspectives toward required tutoring. This work might be appropriately labeled "research" instead of "assessment" because she hoped to gather data that would inform writing centers beyond the context of UAB. The study followed the replicable, aggregable, and data-driven (RAD) model called for by Haswell (2005) and writing center scholars like Driscoll and Perdue (2012), Babcock and Thonus (2012), and Mackiewicz and Thompson (2012).

On the one hand, Jaclyn hoped to address in this project a longstanding question raised by countless writing center practitioners—"What do students think of being required to use the writing center?"—with a study that could be replicated elsewhere to build more knowledge about student perspectives on required tutoring. On the other hand, she wanted to gather data that would help her to understand and immediately shape her own writing center. Specifically, Jaclyn wanted to know what the developmental English course's writing center requirement was doing to student perspectives on the center.

Jaclyn learned from the study that most participants felt positively toward the requirement and the center but felt more positively when their instructors spoke highly of both. The study's findings led to direct, immediate changes. Rather than arguing for discontinuing the requirement, Jaclyn turned her attention toward communicating better about it with students and helping instructors to do the same. For example, she developed a fuller orientation, attended by all developmental English sections early in the semester, that more effectively introduced students and faculty to the center and the requirement.

Communicating with Diverse Stakeholders

As Allen and Jaclyn have described throughout the book, communicating with a variety of stakeholders formed a central part of their work on the CWEST. This work prepared Jaclyn for her current work as a writing center director, as a major part of what she does is communicate with students, faculty, and administrators from all over campus. Additionally, balancing her different roles as a faculty member requires adapting this communication to a variety of stakeholders and purposes. Sometimes, communication reveals conflicts, or at least competing priorities, among Jaclyn's different roles.

As writing center director, for example, Jaclyn faces the regular need to portray the center in the most positive light, a portrayal that is often necessary to promoting services and protecting resources. On the one hand, it's important to avoid the success narrative, but on the other, it's necessary to be very careful about how limitations and failures are discussed. In a time when so many resources like writing centers are facing budget cuts, mergers with other tutoring programs, or even elimination, expressing failure presents risks. Advocates for community-based work face a similar conflict.

Jaclyn most clearly drew this connection between writing centers and community engagement during a meeting of the faculty fellows in service-learning program that she participated in during her second year at UAB. This yearlong program sought to build enthusiasm for community-based work and to equip more faculty members to develop and teach service-learning courses. The program involved monthly meetings with a dozen other fellows and three leaders. Participants developed new service-learning curricula to be taught during the program's second semester or the following year.

Though Jaclyn enjoyed and benefited immensely from the faculty fellows program, she often found that she seemed to worry more than the others about describing the work only in terms of success. This likely resulted from her prior experiences with community engagement, especially the CWEST project. As Jaclyn sat in the classroom during one of the final fellows meetings, she found herself feeling more conflicted than usual about the merits of service-learning.

One of the leaders, the director of engagement at the university, had announced to the group that Jaclyn's service-learning project (taking place that semester) had received media attention. She replied with something like, "I'm surprised that the project has gotten so much attention—it's just a little four-week thing." One of the other leaders, a well-known director of a successful university civic education program, playfully scolded Jaclyn for the way she described the project, saying, "Now look—you can't describe it that way. Do not downplay it."

When Jaclyn laughed him off, he took a more serious tone: "No, really, we *have* to celebrate our service-learning accomplishments. We *have* to get them attention if we expect them to keep going. You *have* to highlight what you have done. You all do." As a fellow administrator, Jaclyn related to the leader's point of view. She realized that his comments, in which he urged faculty to celebrate their service-learning successes instead of drawing attention to their curriculum's limitations, stemmed partly from his role as a longtime advocate of service-learning and administrator of civic engagement programs.

While Jaclyn could understand the program leader's comments as a fellow administrator, as a teacher, she desired more opportunities to examine the challenges and limitations of service-learning. Again, her work in the CWEST project and writing center parallels the differences in her communication and thinking about the work. In courses on tutoring writing and in staff meetings, Jaclyn regularly asks tutors to reflect on the challenging sessions, always returning to the same question: What can we learn from these challenges?

Moreover, Jaclyn regularly assures tutors that a failed session provides as much of an opportunity for learning as a successful session, if not more. While she may emphasize the center's successes and productivity when communicating with "outsiders," Jaclyn focuses regularly on the limitations and challenges of the work with insiders, returning always to how she and the tutors can manage those limitations and learn from their challenges.

In the fellows program, Jaclyn found herself wanting the same types of conversations with other teachers of service-learning. In short, she wanted what she tries to give the tutors in her writing center: a space to discuss candidly the challenges and limitations of service-learning alongside the discussions of its rewards. Jaclyn felt frustrated by the lack of discussion about the perils of service-learning. "It's not perfect," she wanted to say. "It never is."

Managing Expectations and Assuming Future Iterations

In reflecting, Jaclyn realized that her occasional frustration with the faculty fellows program also stemmed from guilt and insecurity about her attempts at service-learning. By the end of the fellows program, Jaclyn had led multiple service-learning projects in courses at several institutions, in addition to her work with the CWEST. She had her share of experience, then, with service-learning and community-based research.

More specifically, by this point in her career, Jaclyn had developed and taught service-learning curricula at Purdue, the University of Southern Indiana, and UAB; she had collaboratively developed and sustained a partnership between a university writing center and two community-based literacy programs for three years; and she had written a dissertation on community-based research and had published the findings. This work was all in addition to several conference presentations and teaching workshops related to service-learning and community engagement and research.

After all of this experience, Jaclyn felt that she should be an expert. She felt that her community-based work should not fail. Unrealistic? Perhaps. But when each of the service-learning projects she ran during and after the CWEST faced challenges and disappointments—and all of them did—she wondered what she really offered to her colleges and communities.

The service-learning project Jaclyn developed during the faculty fellows program offers one example of mixed success. The project emerged from a 200-level place-based writing course called Writing in Birmingham. In the course, students visited a nearby inner-city elementary school to lead third- and fourth-grade children in writing workshops. The project culminated in Jaclyn's students, mainly English majors in professional writing, designing and printing a book of the children's writings.

This project addressed important literacy challenges and offered mutual benefits for the university and community. The elementary school children enjoyed the university students' visits and wrote creatively and happily during the workshops. The school principal expressed enthusiasm for the project and wished that the class would return in the future, and the teachers praised the university students' interaction with the children.

Further, Jaclyn's students got what she hoped they would out of the project, and their formal and informal reflections about the workshops made clear that they cared about the work. The students' writings about the city improved significantly after the project, and they seemed to start thinking about their community in more sophisticated, thoughtful ways. In a course named Writing in Birmingham, this was important.

Returning to that faculty fellows meeting, the one in which Jaclyn bit her tongue for fear of being the squeaky wheel, she worried mainly that the service-learning project had benefited the university more than the community.

More specifically, she worried that the university participants, herself very much included, got more credit than the school got help. For example, the project received more media attention than anyone could have anticipated, which put Jaclyn and her students directly in the spotlight.

The school welcomed the coverage because, as the principal explained, "This school district is usually in the news for all the wrong reasons. This shows the good that does happen in my school." Jaclyn, her students, and the community partners were certainly in the news. By the time everything was said and done, the fairly modest Writing in Birmingham project had been covered in the nightly news on two different channels, had been written about in several online news publications, and had been the focus of a longer piece in the online and print versions of the university magazine.

Jaclyn initially felt thrilled at the attention the project received, especially because of the principal's enthusiasm. As the attention for the project grew, though, she recognized a familiar narrative that made her feel nervous and uncomfortable: Do-gooders from the university go to the "other" part of town to help the poor folks. Perhaps it was Jaclyn's imagination, but this narrative seemed to only get more intense with each story or news spot about the project.

Further, with Birmingham's history of racial violence and current reality of racial tension and discrimination, the authors would be remiss if they did not acknowledge that this narrative took on another dimension: Do-gooder white kids from the university help the poor black children in the city. Similar to Allen's description of Loyola and Baltimore, UAB and Birmingham are fraught with all kinds of racial and socioeconomic tensions. While certainly present in other cities, these tensions can feel even more powerful in a city that still has buildings named after George Wallace.[8]

In addition to lessons about investigating community needs and developing sustainable ways to contribute, Jaclyn regularly needed to relearn two of the main lessons from the CWEST when working on these service-learning projects. First, she relearned that university participants must enter community work with manageable expectations. Second, she relearned that research, assessment, and informal observations should be used to improve future iterations of community-based projects.

A third idea is embedded within these two lessons: There *should* be future iterations of a project. As a teacher, the best advice Jaclyn ever received was to improve rather than throw out lessons, assignments, and course plans. The same is true of community-based work, including both program-based projects like the CWEST and course-based projects like the example described above. Jaclyn's Writing in Birmingham project *did* begin with this idea, and that beginning transformed every failure, challenge, and disappointment into an opportunity to learn for the next time around.

The writing center provides an interesting connection to this type of work. While no writing center director would observe the challenges and limitations of her center and propose starting from the ground up, we regularly do begin again when it comes to teaching and community work. By shifting our perspective on community-based work, including service-learning projects, so that we assume an ongoing engagement, university members can develop more meaningful, sustainable partnerships with the community.

Again, this orientation may mimic that of a writing center; though its open and close dates may follow the academic calendar, a writing center does not stop supporting student writing when the semester ends. A service-learning project may need to end at the semester's close, just as a writing center may need to close for a holiday break. But, faculty members' engagement with the community, and our encouragement of student engagement, can be never finished, just like the writing center. And just like the writing center, we can look for ways to improve constantly, rather than start over constantly.

Finally, while civic engagement is certainly possible in other venues, writing centers can provide stable, long-term spaces for the consistent and empirical work needed for community-based research. Throughout the book, the authors have described the CWEST with the goal of presenting one possibility for such a project. Other projects may look quite different, but the authors hope that the model presented here provides readers ideas for housing engagement in writing centers and drawing from writing center philosophy in community-based engagement and research.

NOTES

1. In his book, *Not in My Neighborhood: How Bigotry Shaped a Great American City*, Antero Pietila (2010) writes, "More than 33,000 homes were foreclosed between 2000 and 2008, when Baltimore became the first city to sue a lender under the 1968 Fair Housing Act. The city accused Wells Fargo of reverse redlining, which was forbidden by the courts. The suit alleged that two-thirds of Wells Fargo's foreclosures in Baltimore were city census tracts that were more than 60 percent African-American while only 15.6 percent were in census tracts that were less than 20 percent black" (p. 258).

2. Blockbusting is defined by W. Edward Orser (1997) as "the intentional action of a real estate operative to settle an African-American household in an all-white neighborhood for the purposes of provoking white flight in order to make excessive profits by buying from those who fled and selling high to those who sought access to new housing opportunities" (p. 4). *Blockbusting in Baltimore: The Edmondson Village Story*.

3. U.S. Census Bureau (2009) American Community Survey 1-Year Estimates: http://www.census.gov/.

4. Bureau of Labor Statistics: http://www.bls.gov/ro3/mdlaus.htm.

5. Final interviews with GEDCO/CARES administrators indicated that the reimbursement amount could be reduced to $20.

6. Throughout this section, the authors draw on the discussion in "Polylog: Are Writing Center Directors Writing Program Administrators?" (2006) published in *Composition Studies*. The authors, including the late Linda Bergmann, resist simple answers to the question but ultimately include leaders from many types of programs, including writing centers, under the umbrella of "writing program administrator." The authors do as well.

7. For more discussion of how community engagement can help graduate students and faculty members prepare for WPA work, please see Jaclyn's "Writing Program Administration and Community Engagement: A Bibliographic Essay," (2010) published in *Going Public: The WPA as Advocate for Engagement*.

8. A former Alabama governor who publically resisted desegregation on multiple occasions.

Epilogue
Looking Back, Looking Forward

The authors began this project just as the 2007 recession began wreaking havoc in the country. As graduate students, Allen and Jaclyn may have been sheltered from the worst of the recession's damage, but they saw evidence of it regularly. As in many Midwestern communities and in towns and cities across the country, to drive through Lafayette meant to drive past vacant homes and shuttered businesses. Panhandlers milled around the Lafayette Greyhound bus stop and downtown shops.

Other markers of the recession were less clearly visible, but unmistakable nonetheless. Nearly everyone knew someone who had lost a job or who was struggling to find work. At Purdue, students worried about whether their mounting student loan debt would be "worth it" when they finished. When the authors taught résumé design to professional writing students, a distinct message, unspoken or not, accompanied the lesson: "There are only *so many opportunities*." That message surfaced more urgently at WorkOne, where clients personally witnessed the decline of employment opportunities.

The detachment between Purdue and Lafayette was unmistakable before, but the recession intensified the feeling of disparity between them. As a state university, Purdue experienced (and continues to experience) the effects of the recession—slashes in funding from Indianapolis are pushing tuition costs higher, and subsequently, more and more of Indiana's families cannot afford to attend their state's land-grant university.

Three years later, the drive off campus in 2010 felt more jarring than ever; it meant driving away from the seemingly never-ending construction of new brick buildings into a downtown that appeared forgotten in the past. The authors occupied a strange space as graduate students. On the one hand, their teaching assistant salaries sent them to the Aldi grocery store for ramen noodles. On the other hand, those modest salaries were at least fairly secure and accompanied by health insurance. More importantly, the authors occupied a position of privilege as educated people with more opportunities than most.

Related to these challenges, the goals for the CWEST project were many. But fundamentally, Jaclyn and Allen hoped to develop relationships that would address some of the disparity they saw between college and community. Though they didn't know exactly how they were going to achieve this goal when the project began, they believed that addressing that disparity through ongoing relationships was the right thing to do.

Recently, Howard Tinberg spoke about these types of civic goals in his 2014 chair's address from the CCCC Convention in Indianapolis. In his address, "The Loss of the Public," Tinberg lamented the lack of attention to public and adult education. In doing so, Tinberg recounted the work of Caleb Mills when he asked, "Am I not interested in the proper education of all that are socially and politically connected to me?" (p. 329).

Though Tinberg (2014) offered a number of strategies to respond to Mills's inquiry, he underscored the value of our field's capability to meet the needs of our communities through "public action . . . service-learning partnerships . . ." and "digital media" (p. 337). Moreover, he reminded us that this type of work is part of our mission, though we still "clearly have our work cut out for us" (p. 337). Tinberg's statements were encouraging, but the authors wonder if enough of our peers are listening or *doing* anything to respond.

Given their interests and background, the authors knew when they began collaborating that they wanted to focus on literacy in the community. And, given their connection to the Purdue OWL, they believed that focusing on Web-based literacy resources made the most sense. As described throughout the book, the authors also knew that they did not want to *serve* the community following a volunteerism or charity model; instead, they wanted to *engage* the community in a more equal, sustainable way that would draw from their own and the community's expertise.

As rhetoric students and writing center tutors, Allen and Jaclyn felt they had something to offer the community, even if they felt less sure of *what* than they might have liked at the beginning of the project. They felt sure, though, that they needed to collaborate with community members who could offer expertise in adult education and local literacy issues. This collaboration would be crucial, as the authors lacked expertise in either of those areas. If necessity is the mother of invention, it's perhaps also the mother of collaboration.

Despite their strong desire to address university-community disparities and their sincere need to collaborate with community members, the authors realize looking back that the CWEST project began with relatively conservative goals. Jaclyn and Allen sought primarily to build relationships with adult literacy educators in the community, and in doing so, they deferred always to their expertise and experience.

Years later, the authors still believe that such respect for community members' knowledge and practices supports university-community relationships, but always deferring to rather than questioning the judgments of project partners can develop conservative aims. Additionally, Allen and Jaclyn still believe that community engagement projects should deliver "real" outcomes for the community, but by focusing exclusively on these outcomes and how they respond to current realities, projects may develop unintentionally conservative goals.

The CWEST project offers one example of how these attentions can create an engagement project with limited objectives. For the CWEST, the authors did not seek to question high-school equivalency opportunities, fight for better resources for the poor, protest that the university owed more to its surrounding community, or make the case that the state or local governments owed more to adult literacy education. Moreover, due to budget restraints at Purdue the authors did not seek to establish satellite centers where Writing Lab tutors could work with local residents.

Despite these limitations, the authors did share the hope with Linda Bergmann that a separate Engagement section on Purdue's OWL might shift people's attention to addressing these issues. Currently, the Purdue rhetoric and composition program is developing more civically engaged graduate courses, and the professional writing and first-year writing programs are both integrating more service-learning. There is even talk of developing an assistant director of civic engagement position within the program.

While the authors clearly cannot take credit for these positive moves, the CWEST was one project in Purdue's rhetoric and composition program and Writing Lab that shifted greater attention to community issues and potential collaborations. Despite this possible impact on their graduate program and writing center, when the authors were in Lafayette, they worked within their limits and attempted merely to expand existing resources, rather than arguing that those resources were fundamentally flawed. In these limited efforts, some success is clear, but so are limitations.

Additionally, the authors attempted to support citizens' ability to pass hurdles for employment and education, rather than making the case that such hurdles were themselves problematic. The GED exam offers perhaps the best example. Early research revealed that GED preparation was one of the most common reasons students studied at LARA. Allen and Jaclyn may have felt a tinge of discomfort when they began their work by purchasing test-preparation books and thinking about how to create resources that perfectly matched the exam's content and format.

During interviews, observations, and casual conversations, though, LARA instructors stated that above all, they showed respect for the *students'* goals; if the students wanted to pass the GED, the teacher's job was to help them do it. Further, many instructors explained—and the authors witnessed at

LARA—that supporting this goal meant studying for the exam specifically, not just the *content* it tested. The authors wanted to respect LARA teachers' philosophy and expertise, so they developed GED materials that offered test-taking strategies and matched the exam's content and structure.

When the authors reflect now, they still believe that this was the right decision. Still, the current situation with those GED resources reveals the limitations of this kind of work. At the time of this writing, the CWEST GED materials were no longer openly available on the Purdue OWL; most pages were removed when Pearson revised the GED in 2014. While the materials could still have helped students study the content tested by the GED exam, it would be irresponsible for a well-known website like the Purdue OWL to have out-of-date resources that contained incorrect information about the exam itself.

Moreover, Purdue Writing Lab staff decided that the LARA ESL resources would better serve users if they were integrated into the rest of the OWL. Again, the authors not only felt conflicted about this change but also realized that writing center staff must compromise and find solutions to the challenging situations they face. Like most people, Jaclyn and Allen look back on their work and feel equal parts pride at what was accomplished and amazement at how much more work there is to do. They both know that the work will never be finished, especially since well-advised changes create new areas of work.

When the CWEST GED materials were removed from the Purdue OWL, the authors were reminded that engagement faces the whims of educational and economic realities beyond our control, but the move also made Allen and Jaclyn question the value of engagement that works within, rather than works to change, existing realities. Rather than develop study materials for the GED exam, should the authors have spent their time fighting for improved high-school equivalency options?

Or, if they still wanted to keep the focus on production, should the authors have insisted on developing literacy materials that helped students learn the content tested by the GED exam, rather than entirely matched its format? Such a decision may have conflicted with the community partners' wishes, but would the authors have done well to question the partners and engage in a more complex, if uncomfortable, conversation about adult literacy education?

Within these types of questions, parallels between community engagement and writing center work become clear. Writing center professionals regularly face a tension between preparing students for the realities of the university and fighting those realities they find problematic. For Jaclyn, one of the hardest questions to answer from a tutor is, "what do I do when I *really* don't agree with an instructor?"

Sometimes, disagreements between instructors and tutors offer valuable moments to show students that there is no one approach to writing. But is it our job to help students meet their instructors' expectations, even when we feel those expectations may be flawed? In a broader sense, is our job to help students pass the hurdles of the university, even when we believe those hurdles may be problematic? Or, is our job to help students question (and question ourselves) the realities they face, including hurdles that they may be desperate to meet for real economic reasons?

If we have answers to these questions in writing center studies, they seem to be "both, and." We hope that we can *both* help students to improve their writing, partly to meet the expectations of the university, *and* use our positions to question the flaws we see in our institutions. The successful tutor and writing center director learns which move each moment requires.

In this sense, the authors argue that writing centers provide ideal locations for community projects and the necessary wisdom to enact such work. The challenges a writing center faces in many ways parallel those that community engagement faces, so those who lead writing centers through these obstacles offer expertise in developing community-based work within the limitations of the university. The authors have already noticed increasing writing center work in civic engagement at conferences, such as the 2015 Conference on Community Writing hosted by the University of Colorado Boulder.

Many scholars have argued that writing centers exist within the currents of broader institutional movements, various theories and pedagogies, conflicting decision-making processes, and even inconsistent revenue streams. That the writing center is already such a multistakeholder, multidisciplinary space presents challenges to building community engagement into its mission, to be sure. But, this reality also means that those who have led and worked in writing centers possess the expertise to support community-based work.

The authors' goal in writing this book was to show how this community work might be possible in one writing center, and they focused on the empirical and iterative process that helped them collaborate with community partners in Lafayette, Indiana. They also focused on the personal relationships that held the CWEST together through the challenges and the small victories that make community-based work so rewarding and important.

Jaclyn's experience as a writing center director since fall 2012 provides an example of both the challenges and advantages administrators and tutors have when developing community-based work. When Jaclyn began the position, her new writing center acted almost entirely as a support for the department's developmental English courses, even though the entrance to the center was adorned with steel letters that read, "*University* Writing Center" (emphasis added).

Jaclyn had a lot of work to do, then. She spent most of her time assessing the center, making changes, promoting its services to various stakeholders, and advocating for increased support. This work took time away from writing center-based community engagement projects. In a sense, Jaclyn simply had to get her "own shop in shape" before she could engage the community beyond the university.

Despite these challenges, Jaclyn has been able to apply her pedagogical and institutional expertise to some community-based work. She developed all of these skills from running a writing center. Jaclyn's community-based work includes the multistakeholder, multisemester service-learning project she describes in chapter 6. It also includes writing workshops and tutoring sessions, through the writing center, for students writing in a variety of service-learning courses, as well as proposing to civic engagement events like the Clinton Global Initiative University.

This second example illustrates Jaclyn's work in gradually building the writing center's role in civic engagement; though she has not yet had the time and resources to develop major community projects based in UAB's writing center, she has had the time and resources to help the center support other community and civic-based projects happening all over the university. Further, after building relationships in the community and university and gradually developing the writing center's reach, the groundwork is set for Jaclyn's center to do more substantial community engagement projects.

To most of our readers, it is not news that writing centers face challenges and competing demands. Writing center administrators like Jaclyn live this reality every day, and they are experienced at thriving within these shifting currents. It is no surprise, therefore, that the 2010 International Writing Centers Association-National Conference on Peer Tutoring in Writing theme was "Safe Harbors or Open Seas?: Navigating Currents in Writing Center Work."

The authors seek to complicate this binary approach: The strengths and experiences that make writing centers successful can help them serve their communities *and* their universities. Rather than forcing choices between supporting and questioning existing realities, those practicing community-based work in writing centers may move amenably between the two. These efforts can be improved by integrating the model presented here, which includes empirical methods, iterative design, and scholarship, but most importantly, personal relationships between university and community members.

However, the authors also recognize that as universities tighten budgets, writing centers may feel pressured to choose between keeping their efforts within the university and developing more projects to support the communities undoubtedly facing similar cutbacks. But Jaclyn and Allen argue that this choice need not be either/or. As shown throughout the book, reaching out from the writing center to communities can generate funding and support university missions while invigorating research and developing reciprocal relationships.

Looking forward, the authors maintain that writing centers offer the wisdom and the experience necessary to building sustained interactions between universities and communities. From what they have heard from peers in writing center studies at gatherings like the Conference on Community Writing, this sort of work is occurring already, is gaining momentum, and is worthy of further study. Allen and Jaclyn feel confident saying, therefore, that writing centers can thrive in *both* the harbor *and* the sea; though not easy, the choice can be both/and.

Appendix
Chapter Heuristic Questions

The authors provide these heuristic questions and research protocols to help readers think critically and creatively about their ideas for civic engagement, to help them move from ideas to actions, and to help them meet their stakeholders' needs.

CHAPTER 1

Getting Started

1. Why are you interested in beginning work with your local community? Why do you value civic engagement? What is your personal instigation?
2. What are your goals? What's your vision for the project? Do your goals and vision align with your institution? Your department? Your program or writing center?
3. Whom does it benefit if your project gets off the ground? Whom might it marginalize or hurt? In what ways? How will you address this?
4. What are the assets and resources you have now that you might leverage to help you begin your project? Would a SWOT (strengths, weaknesses, opportunities, and threats) analysis be helpful to complete? What else do you need?
5. Who are your potential stakeholders and partners within your institution? Within the community?
6. What do you have in common with your potential stakeholders and partners, and how might you build a relationship with these overlaps? Do you share missions and goals? Approaches?

7. What separates you or makes you different from your potential stakeholders and partners? How might you overcome these differences to collaborate?
8. How might you learn more about your potential stakeholders and partners? What past or current projects exist that you might build on?
9. What scholarship in and out of writing studies exists to help guide your work?
10. Who might be able to give you advice from within your discipline? Outside your discipline? Have you consulted Campus Compact resources?

CHAPTER 2

The First Steps

1. What sources do you need to learn more about your stakeholders and partners? What are their histories? Whom do they serve? How are they funded? Who works/volunteers with them? How is their organization structured?
2. At this early stage, who is the best person to meet with to explore partner needs?
3. Is there a need? If so, what are your potential partner's needs? How might you collaborate to build a reciprocal (mutually beneficial) relationship?
4. What type of collaboration might they be interested in? Direct service? Service-learning? Research-driven engaged scholarship? Short term? Long term? Both?
5. What assets and resources do they have that might support collaboration? What else might they need?
6. What other community resources/organizations might get involved to support collaboration?
7. What support/funding resources exist within your institution? Within the local community? Nonprofits? Foundations? What support/funding resources exist within your field? Professional organizations? Will they require grant proposals and/or logic models? (See the W. K. Kellogg Foundation *Logic Model Development Guide*.)
8. If empirical research may be a part of the project, what do you need to do to gain IRB approval? Are the people who may be involved with the research properly certified (CITI, NIH, etc.) to work with human participants and data? What research methods are appropriate and best meet

your partner's needs? Does your partner have an IRB process you will need to follow? Who might help you with an IRB process?
9. Where might you present your work-in-progress to obtain scholarly or peer feedback? Conferences? Research network forums? Workshops? Colloquia? Virtual? Face to face?
10. Where might you submit your work-in-progress to obtain scholarly or peer feedback? Journals? Blogs? Websites?

CHAPTER 3

Collaboration and Feedback

1. Once you have agreed on project goals, responsibilities, and timelines, what process does your partner need to provide feedback? Does this include interviews, focus groups, observations, surveys, other types of methods?
2. Are your community partners comfortable with this type of process? Does it meet their needs?
3. What sort of informed consent process will you need to follow, and are there any at-risk populations or populations with language or disability needs involved?
4. How are you going to recruit and retain participants? How will you reimburse them for their time?
5. How are you going to follow your process? What are the logistics involved? Will there be audio or video recordings? Note taking? Will you need help with this process?
6. How often are you going to collect feedback or data on the project? On the deliverables?
7. How often are you going to revise the process and products based on your partner's feedback?
8. What sort of technology is going to be involved? How are you going to ensure equitable access or use of any technology involved? How will you close a digital divide rather than expanding it?
9. How will you store and maintain your data? Where will it be kept, and who will be responsible for it?
10. Once you begin collecting feedback/data, how will you resist the fate accompli syndrome and other risks to research validity? How might you practice "critical research methods," for example, Sullivan and Porter (1997)?

CHAPTER 4

Iterative Research and Design

1. How might an iterative process of research and development contribute to your project's success? Is this the most effective/appropriate/realistic model for your project?
2. If you are using empirical methods for your project, how are you ensuring that your data collection is following best practices for ethical and effective research?
3. If you are not using empirical methods, how do you plan to assess the progress and outcomes of your project? If you plan to publish on your work, how will you discuss your project in a way your peers will understand and accept your conclusions?
4. If you are using empirical methods, how might you include your community partners in the research process, fostering joint knowledge building?
5. If you are using empirical methods, how do you plan to analyze your data? If appropriate for your project, how do you plan to integrate critical research methods into your analysis?
6. What sort of technologies might help you in your data analysis. (For qualitative data, programs like NVivo might help. For quantitative data, programs like Excel and SPSS might help.)
7. If you are audio or video recording interviews, focus groups, or observations, how will you transcribe this information? Is the transcriptionist an experienced professional that can work with your timeline, budget, and technology requirements? How will you send and receive files? If applicable, does the transcriptionist have experience with dialects or accents?
8. If your project requires multiple researchers, how are you going to divide the data analysis? How will the workflow be shared and organized?
9. If applicable, do you need to norm your data or ensure inter-rater reliability?
10. Do you have a coding scheme and/or coding book you are working with, and if so, how are you organizing it?

CHAPTER 5

Reflections, Assessments, and Outcomes

1. Did the project meet your community partner's needs and expectations? Your stakeholders' needs and expectations?

2. What were the short- and long-term outcomes of your project?
3. How are you determining the outcomes?
4. As you determine and assess outcomes, how do you know your conclusions are as accurate as possible?
5. What are some things you and your partner achieved that you are most proud of? What makes you happiest about your project?
6. What are some things you and your partner could have done more effectively? What are the shortcomings and limitations? What concerns you most about your experiences?
7. What are some of the lessons you learned during your project?
8. How might you apply some of those lessons as you move forward?
9. If appropriate and possible, how might you continue working with your community partner? What do you both need to make that happen?
10. How might you integrate this project into future pedagogy? Future scholarship?

CHAPTER 6

Maintaining Work-Life Balance and Healthy Boundaries

1. Is it appropriate to continue working with your current community partner?
2. Are you meeting your partner's needs and expectations, and can you do so over a long period of time? If not, can the project still be helpful if it runs for a short period of time?
3. In addition to collaborating with the community, are your students/tutors able to fulfill their responsibilities?
4. Are your needs being met? Are you able to fulfill your responsibilities as a teacher? Researcher? Administrator? Caregiver?
5. Are you able to continue your project without sacrificing too much of your personal time? Are you able to continue the project without sacrificing too much of your community partner's personal time?
6. Can you maintain your project without sacrificing your personal money or resources? Can you maintain the project without sacrificing your community partner's personal money or resources?
7. If it is best to pause or end the project, what might be the repercussions of doing so? Whom would it benefit or hurt if the project ended?
8. What stakeholders do you need to speak with to consider pausing or ending the project (your community partner, office of service-learning, foundations, community groups)?
9. Is there anyone with whom you might speak who could help you, someone who has successfully *paused* or *ended* a community engagement project?

10. What are the most effective ways of pausing or ending a project? Is there scholarship from writing studies or other fields (urban studies, public health, psychology, counseling, etc.) on how to do this?

RESEARCH PROTOCOLS

Questions for First LARA Interviews

Question Set 1: General information

1. How long have you been an instructor at LARA?
2. Why do you teach at LARA?
3. How did you become involved with LARA?
4. What is your educational background?
5. Aside from teaching at LARA, what other teaching experiences do you have?
6. What happens during a typical class or tutorial at LARA? What are the classes and/or tutorials like?

Question Set 2: What instructional methods do LARA instructors currently use?

1. What are some strategies you use when working with students who are preparing for the GED?
2. How do your instructional methods differ based on the student you're working with?
3. How much freedom do you have as a LARA instructor to choose methods you use? How much is determined by LARA?
4. Were you ever trained at LARA in certain instructional methods?
5. How do you think your instructional methods differ from those of other instructors?
6. How and when do instructors share teaching strategies with one another?

Question Set 3: What teaching resources are currently available to LARA instructors?

1. What materials are available for you to use during instruction (handouts, PowerPoint presentations, textbooks, etc.)?
2. What materials do you generally use during instruction? What are your reasons for these choices?
3. What types of materials are available for students to use on site?
4. What types of materials are students allowed to take with them?

5. How many computers are available for student and teacher use? Do you typically use computers during your instruction?
6. Do LARA instructors use online resources? What ones? How often? Why or why not?

OBSERVATIONAL PROTOCOL FOR FIRST LARA OBSERVATIONS

Observation Begin/End Time

Content

What is the general subject being taught?
What specific topics are covered during the instruction?
How many different topics are covered?

Materials

What instructional materials are used (textbooks, websites, handouts, etc.)?
How many times does the instructor refer to an instructional resource?
What other materials are used (notebook, scrap paper, computer, chalkboard, etc.)?

Methods

What teaching methods does the instructor use (lecture, group and individual activities, question/answer, etc.)?
How many minutes are spent on each type of activity?

Miscellaneous

How long is the teaching session?
Other observations?

Questions for Second LARA Interviews

Question Set 1: LARA instructors' use of the CWEST

1. How much have you used the CWEST?
2. How do you see yourself using (or how have you used) CWEST resources during instruction?
3. How do you see yourself directing (or how have you directed) students to use CWEST resources?
4. What CWEST resources do you see yourself using (or have you used) most?

5. What CWEST resources do you see yourself using (or have you used) least?
6. How might using CWEST resources require you to alter your teaching strategies?
7. Do you prefer using the CWEST or existing teaching resources that LARA offers?

Question Set 2: LARA instructors' comfort level with the CWEST

1. Are you comfortable using the CWEST? Why or why not?
2. How does your comfort level with the CWEST relate to your comfort with online resources generally?
3. Are you more comfortable using some types of resources than others (e.g., downloadable handouts vs. interactive games)?

Question Set 3: LARA instructors' revisions of the CWEST

1. What do you like about the CWEST?
2. What do you not like?
3. What changes would you make to the CWEST?
4. What have you noticed about your students' response to CWEST materials?

OBSERVATIONAL PROTOCOL FOR SECOND LARA OBSERVATIONS

Observation Begin/End Time

Content

What is the general subject being taught?
What specific topics are covered during the instruction?
How many different topics are covered?

Materials

Aside from the CWEST, are other instructional materials used (textbooks, websites, handouts, etc.)? Which ones? How many times does the instructor refer to them?
What other materials are used (notebook, scrap paper, computer, chalkboard, etc.)?

CWEST Materials

What CWEST materials does the instructor use?
Does the instructor use the online CWEST materials or printed versions?
How does the instructor use the materials?
How many times does the instructor refer to the materials?
How many times does the student refer to the materials?

Methods

What teaching methods does the instructor use (lecture, group and individual activities, question/answer, etc.)?
How many minutes are spent on each type of activity?

Miscellaneous

How long is the teaching session?
Other observations?

CWEST LARA USABILITY TEST PROTOCOL

This protocol is a simple quantitative, task-based protocol combined with a short questionnaire about the experience. The researchers also collected demographic information through a survey.

Note: Make sure each computer has the "home" set to http://owl.english.purdue.edu/engagement. By doing this, the proctor can ask participants to click on the "home" link to proceed to the next task.

The proctor is permitted to repeat the task or clarify questions about the task itself but is not to assist the user or answer questions relating to the navigation of the site as a whole (i.e., the proctor can help participants understand the task but not complete it).

Data Collector Activity: The data collector will record the beginning and end time of the tasks. The data collector will also record the number of clicks that it takes the participant to find the selected information. Timing should begin after the proctor reads the task. Lastly, the data collector will track the navigation pattern and feedback of the participant.

Task Script

Proctor: The computer in front of you is displaying the beginning page of the Purdue OWL's CWEST area. During this phase of the test, we would like you to use the site to find specific information, which will be given to you shortly. You are not going to be evaluated on your proficiency with navigating the Internet or using the computer, rather, this test is to see how well the site allows you to find particular information. We are testing the *site*, not you. Again, participation is voluntary, and you may skip any task or stop the test at any time.

Task 1: Proctor, ask the question: According to the CWEST website, how many parts are there to the language arts writing test of the GED? Answer: Two

> *Data collector:* Record time to completion, number of clicks, navigation, and feedback.
>
> *Proctor:* Ask the participant to return to the CWEST homepage by selecting the browser's "home" button.

Proctor, ask the participant to click on the browser's home button to begin the next task.

Task 2: Proctor, ask the question: According to the CWEST website, how is the GED essay writing test scored? Answer: Using a 4-point holistic scale: 4 (high) to 1 (low): 4. Effective; 3. Adequate; 2. Marginal; 1. Inadequate.

> *Data recorder:* Record time to completion, number of clicks, navigation, and feedback.
>
> *Proctor:* Ask the participant to return to the CWEST homepage by selecting the browser's "home" button.

Task 3: Proctor, ask the question: According to the CWEST website, what steps should you follow to effectively respond to a GED writing prompt? Answer: (1) Read the prompt carefully; (2) underline key words; (3) restate the prompt in your words.

> *Data Recorder:* Record time to completion, number of clicks, navigation, and feedback.
>
> *Proctor:* Ask the participant to return to the CWEST homepage by selecting the browser's "home" button.

Task 4: (speak aloud) Proctor: For this task, we would like you to explain your navigation process and your thoughts about the resources as you're navigating. That is, we would like to know why you're making the choices you're making to try to find the answer to the question. Do you understand what we would like you to do? Ask the question: According to the CWEST website, what are some discourse connectors? Answer: consequently, despite this, therefore, furthermore, in addition, moreover, however, indeed, in fact, nevertheless, then.

> *Data collector:* Record time to completion, number of clicks, navigation, and feedback.
>
> *Proctor:* Ask the participant to return to the CWEST homepage by selecting the browser's "home" button. Then say "Please feel free to explore the CWEST website before you fill out the after-test questionnaire. We're especially interested in what you think about the GED activity game."

After-Test Questionnaire

To be administered directly after the last task is complete.
Participant #: (Date of birth – 09/01/1970) _____
Directions: Please answer the following questions based on your experiences during the computer task.

Finding information on the CWEST site was:
Very difficult | Difficult | Neutral | Easy | Very Easy

Most of the information on the CWEST site was:
Buried deeply in pages | Somewhat buried | Neutral | Accessible | Very accessible

When I was looking for information on the CWEST site, I felt:
Very lost | somewhat lost | Neutral | I knew where I was | I knew exactly where I was

How did you feel when using the CWEST site?:
Very confused | Confused | Neutral | Comfortable | Very comfortable

What features would have helped you find the information faster?
What other changes would you make to the site?

Appendix

LARA INSTRUCTOR INTERVIEW SCRIPT

Participant #: (Date of birth – 09/01/1970) _____

Interview Script

Proctor: This interview is meant to provide information on instructors' experiences with online teaching resources and the CWEST. The interview is also meant to provide information on instructors' expectations of CWEST material. Again, participation is voluntary, and you may skip any question or stop the interview at any time.

Ice Breaker Question: Have you used online teaching material before? What was that like?

1. Now that you've had a chance to surf the CWEST a little, how do you think these resources could be used by LARA instructors and students?
2. What value do you see in the resources from an instructor's point of view? And what do you like about the resources you have seen?
3. What do you think could be improved? Design? Content?
4. How would you measure success or lack of success of the CWEST and its materials?
5. How do you feel about us working with LARA to develop literacy materials?
6. How important is it to you that OWL developers continue to work closely with LARA to generate resources?
7. How important is it to you that the CWEST remain available for LARA use? And how important is it to you that the partnership between the Writing Lab and LARA continue?
8. In observations and interviews with other instructors, we have noticed that working with online resources can sometimes be a challenge. How might you address this? And how important is it to you to have these resources available in print form? Might you use the CWEST resources more if they were in print form?
9. Where do you access the Internet? How important is it to you that you have access to CWEST materials outside LARA?
10. What other resources would you like to see/does LARA need on the CWEST?
11. Lastly, would you be willing to use the CWEST materials to prepare for the GED and submit your practice test scores to see if the materials are helping you?

Other comments:

WORKONE EXPRESS INTERVIEW QUESTIONS

1. What is the purpose/goal/mission of WorkOne Express?
2. Who uses WorkOne? Do you track demographic information? If so, how?
3. If you can say, who funds WorkOne?
4. With the downturn in the economy, have you seen an increase in WorkOne use? How do you track that?
5. What role does writing and writing instruction play in your work?
6. What role do online resources play in your work?
7. Have you used online teaching material before?
8. If you could design writing instruction resources for WorkOne, what would they be and what would they accomplish?
9. What goals do you have for the materials we would like to develop for WorkOne?
10. What purpose do you think these resources will serve?
11. What audience do you think will find these resources valuable? Might these resources be linked to statewide websites/other WorkOne's?
12. What value do you see in the resources from an instructor's point of view?
13. What do you like about the OWL resources you have seen?
14. What do you think could be improved? Design? Content?
15. How would you measure success or lack of success of the CWEST and its materials?
16. How important is it to you that OWL developers work closely with WorkOne to generate resources?
17. How important is it to you that the CWEST remain available for WorkOne use? How important is it to you that the partnership between the Writing Lab and WorkOne continues?
18. How do you think you might use these materials in WorkOne?
19. When may I schedule some observation time?
20. What other LARA/WorkOne people do you think I should interview?

WORKONE EXPRESS USABILITY TESTING

The WorkOne protocols, posttest questions, and demographic survey were similar to the LARA procedures. To save space, we have omitted the WorkOne instruments.

Independent Rater Rubrics

This document evaluation is meant to gather information on résumés and cover letters produced by students at LARA and users of WorkOne Express. Your feedback will help LARA/WorkOne and the Purdue Writing Lab measure the outcomes of a new collaborative project that focuses on helping people improve workplace and life skills literacy. We will use this information to help improve the literacy program resources to better serve LARA/WorkOne instructors' needs and the needs of their students/users. Your feedback will help improve instruction, and it may help LARA/WorkOne students/users move successfully into the workplace. Again, participation is voluntary, and you may skip any question or stop the document review at any time. Thank you for your help.

Résumé

Document Design

Résumé appearance makes it easy to read:
Strongly disagree | Disagree | Neutral | Agree | Strongly agree

Résumé headings, layout, and white space are effective:
Strongly disagree | Disagree | Neutral | Agree | Strongly agree

Content

Résumé objective is clear:
Strongly disagree | Disagree | Neutral | Agree | Strongly agree

Résumé education section is clear:
Strongly disagree | Disagree | Neutral | Agree | Strongly agree

Résumé work experience section is clear:
Strongly disagree | Disagree | Neutral | Agree | Strongly agree

Résumé references section is clear (if applicable): Circle if not provided: N/A
Strongly disagree | Disagree | Neutral | Agree | Strongly agree

Résumé indicates author is qualified:
Strongly disagree | Disagree | Neutral | Agree | Strongly agree

Is there any missing information? If so, what is it?
Do you have any specific (positive or negative) comments on this document?
Do you have any suggestions on how to improve this document?

Appendix

Cover Letter

Document Design

Letter appearance makes it easy to read:
Strongly disagree | Disagree | Neutral | Agree | Strongly agree

Letter headings, layout, and white space are effective:
Strongly disagree | Disagree | Neutral | Agree | Strongly agree

Content

Letter address section is clear:
Strongly disagree | Disagree | Neutral | Agree | Strongly agree

Letter introduction explains author's objective and shows author's willingness to help organization:
Strongly disagree | Disagree | Neutral | Agree | Strongly agree

Letter body paragraphs explain author's qualifications, abilities, and experience:
Strongly disagree | Disagree | Neutral | Agree | Strongly agree

Letter closing is professional and provides contact information:
Strongly disagree | Disagree | Neutral | Agree | Strongly agree

Letter indicates author is qualified:
Strongly disagree | Disagree | Neutral | Agree | Strongly agree

Is there any missing information? If so, what is it?
Do you have any specific (positive or negative) comments on this document?
Do you have any suggestions on how to improve this document?
How likely are you to give the author an interview (5 being most likely)?:
1 | 2 | 3 | 4 | 5
Why *would* you interview this person?—Or—Why *wouldn't* you interview this person?

References

About the standards (2015). Common Core State Standards Initiative. Retrieved from http://www.corestandards.org/.
Asen, R. (2004). A discourse theory of citizenship. *Quarterly Journal of Speech* 90(2), 189–211.
Babcock, R. D., and Thonus, T. (2012). *Researching the writing center: Towards an evidence-based practice.* New York: Peter Lang.
Baltimore City View (2015). Baltimore City Government. Retrieved from http://cityview.baltimorecity.gov/CityView/.
Bergmann, L. S. (2010). The writing center as site for engagement. In S. K. Rose and I. Weiser (eds), *Going public: What writing programs can learn from engagement* (pp. 160–76). Logan, UT: Utah State University Press.
Bergmann, L. S., Wells, J. M., and Brizee, A. (2012). The engaged dissertation: Three points of view. In C. Martin and G. Wright (eds), *Collaborative futures: Critical reflections on publicly active graduate education* (pp. 229–57). Syracuse, NY: Graduate School Press, Syracuse University.
Bishop, W. (1990). Bringing writers to the center: Some survey results, surmises, and suggestions. *The Writing Center Journal 10*(2), 31–45.
Bloom, L. Z. (2002). Are we having fun yet?: Necessity, creativity, and writing program administration. *WPA: Writing Program Administration 26*(1/2), 57–70.
Bowden, M., and Scott, J. B. (2003). *Service-learning in technical and professional communication.* New York: Longman.
Boyer, E. L. (1990). *Scholarship reconsidered: Priorities of the professoriate.* The Carnegie Foundation for the Advancement of Teaching. San Francisco, CA: Jossey-Bass.
Brizee, A. (2014). Toward participatory civic engagement: Findings and implications of a three-year community-based research study. *Computers and Composition: An International Journal 32*, 22–40.
Brizee, A., Sousa, M., and Driscoll, L. (2012). Writing centers and students with disabilities: The user-centered approach, participatory design, and empirical research

as collaborative methodologies. *Computers and Composition: An International Journal* 29(4), 341–66.

Charlton, C., Charlton, J., Graban, T. S., Ryan, K. J., and Stolley, A. F. (2011). *GenAdmin: Theorizing WPA identities in the twenty-first century.* Anderson, SC: Parlor Press.

Coe, M. (1996). *Human factors for technical communicators.* New York: Wiley & Sons.

Condon, F. (2009). The pen pal project. *Praxis: A Writing Center Journal* 2(1), n.p. Retrieved from http://www.praxisuwc.com/.

Connaster, B. R. (1999). Last rites for readability formulas in technical communication. *Journal of Technical Writing and Communication* 29(3), 271–87.

Coogan, D. (2005). Counterpublics in public housing: Reframing the politics of service learning. *College English* 67(5), 461–82.

Cushman, E. (1996). The rhetorician as an agent of social change. *College Composition and Communication* 47(1), 7–26.

———. (1999). The public intellectual, activist research, and service-learning. *College English* 61(3), 328–36.

———. (2002). Sustainable service learning programs. *College Composition and Communication* 54, 40–65.

Cushman, E., and Grabill, J. T. (2008/2009). Writing theories/changing communities: Introduction. *Reflections: A Journal of Public Rhetoric, Civic Writing, and Service Learning* 8(3), 1–17.

Deans, T. (2010). English studies and public service. In T. Deans, B. Roswell, and A. J. Wurr (eds), *Writing and community engagement: A critical sourcebook* (pp. 97–116). Boston: Bedford/St. Martin's.

Dewey, J. M. (2012). Search for the great community. *The public and its problems.* University Park, PA: Penn State Press.

Driscoll, D., and Perdue, S. W. (2012). Theory, lore, and more: An analysis of RAD research in *The Writing Center Journal*, 1980–2009. *The Writing Center Journal* 32(1), 11–39.

Dubinsky, J. M. (2002). Service-learning as a path to virtue: The ideal orator in professional communication. *Michigan Journal of Community Service Learning* 8, 61–74.

Duffy, T. M. (1985). Readability formulas: What's the use? In T. M. Duffy and R. Waller (eds), *Designing usable texts* (pp. 113–43). Orlando, FL: Academic Press.

Dumas, J. S., and Redish, J. C. (1999). *A practical guide to usability testing.* Wiltshire: Cromwell Press.

Edbauer, J. (2005). Unframing models of public distribution: From rhetorical situation to rhetorical ecologies. *Rhetoric Society Quarterly* 35(4), 5–25.

Ehn, P. (1992). Scandinavian design: On participation and skill. In P. S. Adler and T. A. Winograd (eds), *Usability: Turning technologies into tools* (pp. 96–132). New York: Oxford University Press.

Flower, L. (2008). *Community literacy and the rhetoric of public engagement.* Carbondale, IL: Southern Illinois University Press.

Grabill, J. T. (2007). *Writing community change: Designing technologies for citizen action.* Cresskill, NJ: Hampton Press.

Greenwood, D. J., and Levin, M. (2003). Reconstructing the relationships between universities and society through action research. In N. K. Denzin and Y. S. Lincoln (eds), *The landscape of qualitative research: Theories and issues* (pp. 85–106). 2nd edition. Thousand Oaks, CA: Sage Publications.

Harry, D. (2010). *Facing the center: Toward an identity politics of one-to-one mentoring*. Logan, UT: Utah State University Press.

Haswell, R. H. (2005). NCTE/CCCC's recent war on scholarship. *Written Communication 22*, 198–223.

Heath, S. B. (2006). *Ways with words: Language, life, and work in communities and classrooms*. Cambridge, UK: Cambridge University Press.

Hesse, D. (1999). The WPA as husband, father, ex. In D. George (ed), *Kitchen cooks, plate twirlers, and troubadours: Writing program administrators tell their stories* (pp. 44–55). Portsmouth, NH: Heinemann.

Hwang, W., and Salvendy, G. (2010). Number of people required for usability evaluation: The 10± rule. *Communications of the ACM 53*(5), 130–33.

Ianetta, M., Bergmann, L., Fitzgerald, L., Haviland, C. P., Lebduska, L., and Wislocki, M. (2006). Polylog: Are writing center directors writing program administrators? *Composition Studies 34*(2), 11–42.

Indiana K–12 Education Data (2009). Indiana Department of Education. Retrieved from http://www.doe.in.gov/.

Jesson, J. (2006). Professional development and the community writing center. *Praxis: A Writing Center Journal 4*(1), n.p. Retrieved from http://www.praxisuwc.com/.

Johnson, R. (1998). *User-centered technology: A rhetorical theory for computers and other mundane artifacts*. Albany, NY: State University of New York Press.

Kellogg Commission (2001). *Returning to our roots: Executive summaries of the reports of the Kellogg Commission on the future of state and land-grant universities*. Washington, DC: National Association of State Universities and Land-Grant Colleges. Retrieved from http://www.aplu.org/.

Lafayette Adult Resource Academy Website (2007). Lafayette Adult Resource Academy. Retrieved from http://www.laralafayette.org/.

Lafayette Urban Enterprise Association Website (2015). Lafayette Urban Enterprise Association. Retrieved from http://luea.org/.

LARA/WorkOne Yearly Report (2008). Lafayette Adult Resource Academy. Yearly report. Lafayette, IN.

Leon, K., and Sura, T. (2013). "We don't need any more brochures": Rethinking deliverables in service learning curricula. *WPA: Writing Program Administration 36*(2), 59–74.

Lerner, N. (1997). Counting beans and making beans count. *The Writing Lab Newsletter 22*, 1–4.

Mackiewicz, J., and Thompson, I. K. (2014). *Talk about writing: The tutoring strategies of experienced writing center tutors*. New York: Routledge.

Mathieu, P. (2005). *Tactics of hope: The public turn in English composition*. Portsmouth, NH: Boynton/Cook Publishers.

Mazur, B. (2000). Revisiting plain language. *Technical Communication 47*(2), 205.

Nielsen, J. (2005). *Beyond accessibility: Treating users with disabilities as people*. Retrieved from https://www.nngroup.com/.

Ornatowski, C., and Bekins, L. (2004) What's civic about technical communication? Technical communication and the rhetoric of "community." *Technical Communication Quarterly 13*(3), 251–69.

Orser, E. (1994). *Blockbusting in Baltimore*. Lexington, KY: State University of Kentucky.

Pietila, A. (2010). *Not in my neighborhood: How bigotry shaped a great American city*. Chicago, IL: Ivan R. Dee.

Redish, J., and Seltzer, J. (1985). The place of readability formulas in technical communication. *Technical Communication 32*(4), 46–52.

Rose, M. (2012). *Back to school: Why everyone deserves a second chance at education*. New York: The New Press.

Rumsey, S. K., and Nihiser, T. (2010, 2011). Expectation, reality, and rectification: The merits of failed service learning. *Community Literacy Journal 5*(2), 135–51.

Schendel, E., and Macauley, W. J., Jr. (2012). *Building writing center assessments that matter*. Logan, UT: Utah State University Press.

Schriver, K. A. (1993). Quality in document design: Issues and controversies. *Technical Communication 40*(2), 239.

Simmons, M. W., and Grabill, J. T. (2007). Toward a civic rhetoric for technologically and scientifically complex places: Invention, performance, and participation. *College Composition and Communication 58*(3), 419–48.

———. (2008). *Participation and power: Civic discourse in environmental policy decisions*. Albany, NY: SUNY Press.

Strauss, A. L. (1987). *Qualitative analysis for social scientists*. New York: Cambridge University Press.

Sullivan, P. A., and Porter, J. E. (1997). *Opening spaces: Writing technologies and critical research practices*. Greenwich, CT: Ablex Publishing Corporation.

Tecumseh Area Partnership Website (2008). Tecumseh Area Partnership. Retrieved from http://www.region4workforceboard.org/.

Theofanos, M. F., and Redish, J. (2005). Helping low-vision and other users with websites that meet their needs: Is one site for all feasible? *Technical communication 52*(1), 9–20.

Tinberg, H. (2014). 2014 CCCC Chair's address: The loss of the public. *College Composition and Communication 66*(2), 327–41.

Wagner-Peyser Act (2009). U.S. Department of Labor. Retrieved from https://www.doleta.gov/programs/w-pact_amended98.cfm.

Wells, J. M. (2010). Writing program administration and community engagement: A bibliographic essay. In S. Rose and I. Weiser (eds), *Going public: The WPA as advocate for engagement* (pp. 237–55). Logan, UT: Utah State University Press.

———. (2014). Investigating adult literacy programs through community engagement research: A case study. *Community Literacy Journal 8*(2), 49–67.

WorkOne West Central Website (2009). WorkOne West Central. Retrieved from http://www.workonewestcentral.org/.

Index

ABE. *See* adult basic education
ACT's KeyTrain and WorkKeys, 33, 78
Adobe Flash, 52, 61n4
adult basic education (ABE), 15–16, 24, 25, 27, 45. *See also* Lafayette Adult Resource Academy (LARA)
Alcoa, 33
Alice (LARA teacher), 54–56, 57–58
Allen. *See* Brizee, Allen
Alpha Phi Omega (APO), 6
Amanda (WorkOne client), 76–77
Anderson, Wes, 8
Ann (LARA teacher), 46–48, 57–60
APO. *See* Alpha Phi Omega
"Are We Having Fun Yet? Necessity, Creativity, and Writing Program Administration" (Bloom), 117
assessment, 27, 81–83, 83n3, 118–19
Audrey (LARA teacher), 70

Babcock, R. D., 119
Bacha, Jeffrey, 51, 63, 66
Back to School: Why Everyone Deserves a Second Chance at Education (Rose), 2, 14, 89
"Basic Skills Improvement program," 27
Bergmann, Linda, 18, 20, 37, 45, 106, 117, 125n6; on CWEST engagement section, 65; on project cost, 39–40; on project stakeholders, 22–23, 25–26; as writing center scholar, 3
Beth (quasi-experiment participant), 82
Betty (LARA teacher), 92–94
Blackmon, Samantha, 52
blockbusting, 108, 113, 124n2
Blockbusting in Baltimore: The Edmondson Village Story (Orser), 124n2
Bloom, Lynn Z., 117
Bowden, Melody, 3, 108–9
Boyer, Ernest L., 105–6, 112, 116, 119
"break bread," 73–74, 114
Brizee, Allen, 1, 83n5, 85; adult literacy as motivation for, 15–16; Amanda conversation with, 76–77; Art of Rhetoric class of, 110; capstone project proposal of, 34–35; community-based research approach of, 5; community members collaboration of, 128–29; on Cub Scouts and civic responsibility, 9–10; CWEST collaboration of, 3–4, 13; CWEST emergent methodology of, *19*, 19–20, *21*, *86*, *105*; CWEST final reflections of, 102–3; CWEST project maps of, 22–23, *22–23*; CWEST role of, 18; CWEST usability testing of, 65, 67;

155

early education of, 10; education path of, 94–95; end-user participants need of, 97–98; engaged scholarship model of, *107*, 115; on first day at Bryant, 10–11; first usability testing day at LARA of, 95–97; focus on literacy in community of, 128; GED pretest experience of, 11; generation one test findings of, 69–71; generation two testing of, 79, *80*; grounded theory use of, 69, 70, 112; IRB challenges of, 38–39; on LARA connection, 12–13; LARA first meeting of, 24–25; LARA tutoring of, 99–102; Lawrence conference with, 100–101; lessons learned by, 103–4; Loyola University Maryland teaching responsibilities of, 106; NOVA experience of, 11–12; praxis-oriented approach of, 9–10; revision of generation one test findings of, 71–72; Rhetoric of Professional Writing class of, 110; stage one and two budget of, 40; Sunrise Diner meeting with Sam, 73–76; Technical Writing class of, 110; on VT service-learning project, 12; WorkOne developing resources by, 78–79; workplace and job search resources responsibility of, 43–44; Writing for the Web class of, 110; YRLEI coding and analyzing of data by, 112; YRLEI project of, 108–12; YRLEI strategies of, 112–15
Bryant Adult Education Center, 10–11, 94–95, 99–101
Bryant Alternative High School, 10
budget: of CWEST, 40; LARA's limited, 46; for WorkOne Express, 33; for YRLEI, 110–11
Building Writing Center Assessments that Matter (Schendel and Macauley), 119

Caranante, Giuliana, 110–13
Caterpillar, 33, 74

CCCC. *See* Conference on College Composition and Communication
Charlton, C., 116, 117
Cimasko, Tony, 43, 67, 68
civic engagement, 3, 5, 12, 37–38, 101–2, 105–9, 115; Brizee early lessons in, 10; needs and willingness in, 16, 18; positives and negatives in, 34, 97–98; writing centers role in, 124, 129, 131–32
Clinton Global Initiative University, 132
collaboration, 2–4, 13–14, 41, 101, 110, 128–29, 133
community-based research, 5, 20, 38–39, 85, 89–90, 95, 122; flexibility in, 94; inherent challenges to, 97–99; interdisciplinary possibilities of, 112; key takeaways from, 103–4; writing centers regarding, 104, 124, 131; YRLEI as, 109–10
community engagement, 1–2, 85; challenges to, 3; educators lack of, 3; pitfalls of, 4–5; writing center connection with, 120, 130–31
Community Literacy and the Rhetoric of Public Engagement (Flower), 5
Community Writing and Education Station (CWEST), 14, 85–86, 89, 95; adult education context differs from university context in, 45; adult literacy as motivation for, 15–16; attention to community issues in, 129; Brizee and Wells collaboration on, 3–4, 13; Brizee and Wells's roles in, 18; collaborative knowledge building used in, 36; community members meetings for, 16; computer access conundrum of, 47–48; conversations about, 22; data analysis of, 69; demographics of test participants in, 68–69; digital and print resources consideration in, 55–56; emergent methodology of, *19*, 19–20, *21*, 86, *105*; engagement section of OWL in, 63–64; final methodology steps of, *86*; final

reflections on, 102–3; funding opportunities for, 40–41; GED Essay Game in, 52, *53*, 54, 61n4, 93; GED revision affecting, 130; generation one test findings of, 69–71; generation one testing process of, *68*; generation two testing of, 79, *80*; guided and independent instructional resources of, 57–58; Halo and Subject and Research Expectancy effects in, 98, 99; Hawthorne and Reverse Hawthorne effects in, 98; interactive level-appropriate resources in, 59; IRB process of, 37–39; jail use of GED section in, 55; key takeaways from, 103–4; LARA and WorkOne use of, 101–2; LARA first meeting about, 24–25; limitations of, 129; mixed-methods methodological framework of, 5, 36; motivation for, 1; as needs-based project, 23; organization of area on OWL, 65–66; original formation of, 2; power dynamic limitation of, 98–99; project maps of, 22–23, *22–23*; project timeline of, 35–36; qualitative methods in, 37; reading level in, 66; recursive processes of, 44; research methods used in, 67–68; research on adult literacy and job resources for, 16; revisable resources for, 60; revision of generation one test findings of, 71–72; stage one and two budget of, 40; stakeholder participation in, 37–38; statistics shaping project of, 2; "swooping" avoidance in, 5; taxonomy original and revised of, *72*; three target areas of, 43; transferable resources of, 58–59; UAB writing center influence of, 118, 120, 123; usability concerns of, 65, 114; WorkOne usability findings on, 80–81; YRLEI project guided by, 108–9. *See also* ESL section; GED section

Compass test, 58

Condon, Frankie, 3
Conference on College Composition and Communication (CCCC), 128
Conference on Community Writing, University of Colorado, Boulder, 131, 133
Coogan, David, 2–3, 5
Crews, Robin, 106
Cushman, Ellen, 2–3, 5, 13
CWEST. *See* Community Writing and Education Station

data analysis and tracking, 67–71, 83n2, 110–12, 115, 119
Deans, Thomas, 3, 5
Department of Defense, U. S., 12
Department of Workforce Development, 31
descriptive statistical analysis, 69
Diane (test participant), 70
Driscoll, Dana, 37, 63, 65, 68, 96–97, 119
Dubinsky, Jim, 5, 12
Dumas, J. S., 69

Edbauer, Jenny, 4
Ehn, Pelle, 37–38, 51
Elaine (LARA teacher), 57–59
emergent methodology, *19*, 19–20, *21*, *86*, *105*
engaged scholarship model, 105–6, *107*, 112, 115–16, 119
English as a Second Language (ESL), 15, 17, 27, 33, 35, 39, 44; Cimasko expertise in, 43, 67
"English Studies and Public Service" (Deans), 5
ESL. *See* English as a Second Language
ESL section, 43, 130; Cimasko drafting of, 66; generation one test of, 67–71

Fairfield Township Trustees, 33
Fair Housing Act, 124n1
first-year composition (FYC), 106
Flesch-Kincaid readability score, 66
Flower, Linda, 3, 5, 85

funding, 3, 27–30, 40–41
FYC. *See* first-year composition

GEDCO/CARES. *See* Govans Ecumenical Development Corporation
GED section, 11, 44, 56, 99–102, 129–30; essay materials included in, 49; "exercises" in, 52; feedback to, 49–51; first drafts of, 49, 50; GED Essay Game in, 52, *53*, 54, 61n4, 93; generation one test of, 67–71; instructors use of, 54; interactive level-appropriate resources in, 59; iterative steps for, *43*; jail use of, 55; LARA software of, 46; LARA student population revising of, 51; major criticisms of, 50; multiple-choice section of, 49; OWL organization strategies for, 51; OWL removal of, 89; OWL resources lack in, 25, 41n2, 43, 60n1; readability improved in, 51; revisable resources for, 60; revision of, 130; transferable resources of, 58–59; Wells materials drafting of, 48–49, 86–87; writing part of, 48–49, 61n3
GenAdmin: Theorizing WPA Identities in the Twenty-First Century (Charlton), 116, 117
Goldblatt, Eli, 3
Govans Ecumenical Development Corporation (GEDCO/CARES), 109, 113–14; YRLEI data tracking of, 112; YRLEI usability testing and workshops of, 110
Grabill, Jeffrey, 3, 5, 36, 51
Great Depression, 31
Greenwood, D. J., 88–90, 92
grounded theory, 69, 70, 112

Halo and Subject and Research Expectancy effects, 98, 99
Haswell, R. H., 119
Hawthorne and Reverse Hawthorne effects, 98

Hayfield Junior High and High School, Fairfax County, Virginia, 10, 100
Heilker, Paul, 3
Hesse, Doug, 117–18
"hit-it-and-quit it," 5

ILR. *See* Instructional Learner Record
"imposter syndrome," 7, 12
independent raters of résumés, 82, 83n4, 102
Indiana Department of Workforce Development, 32
institutional review board (IRB), 20–21, 35–39, 98
Instructional Learner Record (ILR), 29
International Writing Centers Association, 132
IRB. *See* institutional review board
iterative design, 20, 37, 41, *43*, 71–72, 75–76, 132

Jaclyn. *See* Wells, Jaclyn M.
Jesson, James, 3
Joan (LARA teacher), 46, 57–59
JobWorks, Inc., 32
Johnson, Robert, 5
Journal and Courier newspaper, 32

Karen (quasi-experiment participant), 82
"Keep Austin Weird" campaign, 4
Knox College, 6

Lafayette, Indiana: community engagement lack in, 2; public school performance in, 2, 14–15; Purdue distance between, 13–14, 128; recession affects on, 127
Lafayette Adult Reading Academy, 27–28, 41
Lafayette Adult Resource Academy (LARA), 15, 20–21, 41, 66, 85; Adult Education Personnel by Function and Job Status of, 28, *29*; beginnings of, 26–27; Brizee first usability testing day at, 95–97; Brizee's connection with, 12–13;

Brizee tutoring at, 99–102; building and area surrounding, 17; CD and PDF resources for, 47, 55; computer use instruction time of, 57–58; CWEST use of, 101–2; determining needs and willingness of, 16, 18; digital and print resource use at, 55–56; diverse teaching and learning styles at, 45–46; flexible resource needs of, 54–55; GED preparation at, 129–30; GED revising for student population at, 51; GED software in, 46; history of change in, 26–28; "How LARA is Funded" handout, 27, 28; ILR of, 29; individualized instruction and flexibility level of teachers at, 46; Internet access in, 46–47; key partnerships of, 31; limited budget at, 46; limited resources of students at, 47; location of, 26; longstanding role of, 16–17; name changes of, 27, 41n3; needs assessment and findings of, 27; new teaching context writing for, 86–88; objectives as crucial in funding of, 29–30; online and digital resources reactions at, 46; online resource print option need of, 70; outreach mission of, 30; project proposal to, 35; Purdue OWL interest and use of, 24–25, 98–99; Purdue Writing Lab differences and similarities with, 30, 45, 87; "Reading Academy" of, 26; research on, 23–24; state and federal funding of, 27; supplemental funding of, 27–28; teacher and staff use of technology at, 65; teaching context of, 44–45, 87; technology use of clients at, 64–65; updated resources for, 64; Wells action research of, 88–89; Wells's first encounter with, 8–9; Wells's first observation of, 90–92; Wells's jail branch observation and participation in, 92–94; WorkOne partnership with, 31

Lafayette Community Development, 33
Lafayette School Corporation (LSC), 27
Lafayette Urban Enterprise Association (LUEA), 31, 33
LARA. *See* Lafayette Adult Resource Academy
Lawrence (LARA student), 100–101
Leon, K., 25
Lerner, N., 118
Levin, M., 88–90, 92
Likert scale, 37, 68, 69, 71
"The Loss of the Public" (Tinberg), 128
"Loyola is Listening" campaign, 108, 112
Loyola University Maryland, 106, 109
LSC. *See* Lafayette School Corporation
LUEA. *See* Lafayette Urban Enterprise Association

Macauley, W. J., Jr., 119
Mackiewicz, J., 119
Mavis Beacon Teaches Typing, 33, 78
Mills, Caleb, 128
mixed-methods and iterative process, 5, 36, 63, *63*; qualitative data areas in, 67–68, 70; quantitative data areas in, 68, 70–71, 83n2
Moe, Alden, 26–27

National Conference on Peer Tutoring in Writing, "Safe Harbors or Open Seas?: Navigating Currents in Writing Center Work," 132
National Writing Project (NWP), 3
New Media Studio course, 52
Northern Virginia Community College (NOVA), 11
Not in My Neighborhood: How Bigotry Shaped a Great American City (Pietila), 124n1
NOVA. *See* Northern Virginia Community College
NWP. *See* National Writing Project

Online Writing Lab, Purdue (OWL), 16, 18, 41, 44, 50, 88, 102; CWEST section of, 63–66; engagement section of, 129; GED resources lack on, 25, 41n2, 43, 60n1; GED revised posting on, 54, 56; GED section removal of, 89, 130; interactive resource problem of, 52; LARA interest and use of, 24–25, 98–99; mixed-methods and iterative process of, 63, *63*; three-tiered taxonomy of, 66; usability of, 51, 56, 60; web-based literacy resources focus of, 128; WorkOne revised posting on, 79

Opening Spaces (Sullivan and Porter), 23

Orser, W. Edward, 124n2

"the other side," 2, 73

OWL. *See* Online Writing Lab, Purdue

Pearson, 130
Pepper, Mark, 52
Perdue, S. W., 119
Pietila, Antero, 124n1
Porter, J. E., 1, 23
public rhetoric course, 97; end-of-term presentation for, 36; public school performance article of, 2, 14–15
Purdue University, 1, 7, 12; Academy Park development of, 17; improve local education collaboration of, 2, 14; Lafayette distance between, 13–14, 128; recession affects on, 127; service learning projects of, 4–5, 16; student resources at, 47; university-community boundaries in, 2, 13

RAD. *See* replicable, aggregable, and data-driven model

"Reconstructing the Relationships between Universities and Society through Action Research" (Greenwood and Levin), 88

recruitment, 39, 104, 112, 113–14
Redish, J. C., 69
redlining, 108, 113, 124n1

Rensselaer Polytechnic Institute (RPI), 13–14

replicable, aggregable, and data-driven (RAD) model, 119

resources, 16, 33, 43–44, 46, 64, 78–79, 128; CD and PDF, 47, 55; digital and print, 55–56; guided and independent instructional, 57–58; interactive level-appropriate, 59; OWL's lack of GED, 25, 41n2, 43, 60n1; revisable, 60; transferable, 58–59

résumés, 6, 16, 32–33, 36, 98, 102, 114; measuring outcomes of, 81–82, 83n3; print resources for, 76, 79

"The Rhetorician as an Agent of Social Change" (Cushman), 13

Richnor Springs Neighborhood Association (RSNA), 109–10

Robert E. Lee High School, 10, 100
Roosevelt, Franklin D., 31
Rose, Mike, 2, 14–15, 89
Rosetta Stone, 33, 78
RPI. *See* Rensselaer Polytechnic Institute
RSNA. *See* Richnor Springs Neighborhood Association

Sally (LARA volunteer), 75, 77, 79, 81
Sam (WorkOne site coordinator), 31, 33, 79; on "breaking bread," 73–74; Sunrise Diner meeting of, 73–76; technology skills of, 76
Schendel, E., 119
Scott, J. Blake, 3, 108–9
"second-chance institutions," 12, 14–15, 89
service-learning, 12, 20, 38, 73, 129; courses of, 25, 108, 120; instructors questions in, 85; other projects of, 97, 107, 110, 112, 128; problems in, 5; Purdue projects in, 4–5, 16; Wells regarding, 121–24, 132; YRLEI as, 109

"Service-Learning as a Path to Virtue: The Ideal Orator in Professional Communication" (Dubinsky), 5
Service-Learning in Technical and Professional Communication (Bowden and Scott), 108
Seyler, Dorothy, 11
Simmons, Michele, 3, 5, 36, 51
stakeholders, 22–23, 25–26, 37–38, 120–21
Strauss, Anselm, 69
Subaru of Indiana Automotive, 33, 74
Sullivan, Patricia, 1–2, 14–16, 18, 22–23, 25–26, 97
Sunrise Diner, 73, 74, 76, 86, 114
Sura, T., 25
Susan (LARA teacher), 91
"Sustainable Service Learning Programs" (Cushman), 5
Suzanne (LARA administrator), 23–25, 29, 41n1
"swooping," 5

TAP. *See* Tecumseh Area Partnership
technology, 4; LARA staff and client use of, 64–65; Sam's skills in, 76; WorkOne staff and client use of, 76–78; YRLEI addressing of skills in literacy and, 112–13
Tecumseh Area Partnership (TAP), 31, 33
Tecumseh Junior High School Annual Essay Contest, 18
Thompson, I. K., 119
Thonus, T., 119
Tinberg, Howard, 128
Tippecanoe County Correctional Facility, 74
"Toward a Civic Rhetoric for Technologically and Scientifically Complex Places" (Simmons and Grabill), 5, 36
"townies," 7, 14
Troy, New York, 13–14
tutoring, 12, 18, 30, 94, 99–102, 119–21, 132

UAB. *See* University of Alabama, Birmingham
UAB writing center, 115–16, 124; "bean-counting" in, 118; community engagement connection with, 120; CWEST project influence in, 118, 120, 123; diverse stakeholder communication in, 120–21; early assessment of, 118; focused assessment in, 119; over attachment to, 117–18; RAD model study of, 119–20; usage increase in, 118; Wells as director of, 117–19, 132; Writing in Birmingham service-learning project of, 122–23. *See also* writing centers
United States Office of Education's Right to Read Initiative, 26
United Way, 27, 33
University of Alabama, Birmingham (UAB), 115
University of Utah "University Neighborhood Partners" program report, 3
"Urban Enterprise Zone," 17
usability testing, 65, 67, 95–97, 110
The User-Centered Approach (Johnson), 5

Virginia Tech (VT), 12

Wabash River, 2, 14, 73
Wagner-Peyser Act, 31
Wallace, George, 123, 125n8
Washington Elementary School, 17, 31, 73–74, 95
"We Don't Need Any More Brochures: Rethinking Deliverables in Service-Learning Curricula" (Sura and Leon), 25
Wells, Jaclyn M., 1, 5, 85, 125n7; action research of, 88–89; adult literacy as motivation for, 15–16; capstone project proposal of, 34–35; community comfort level of, 86; community members collaboration of, 128–29; CWEST collaboration

of, 3–4, 13; CWEST emergent methodology of, *19*, 19–20, *21*, *86*, *105*; CWEST final reflections of, 102–3; CWEST project maps of, 22–23, *22–23*; CWEST role of, 18; early college experience of, 6–7; first LARA observation of, 90–92; first usability testing day at LARA of, 95–97; focus on literacy in community of, 128; GED materials drafting and revision of, 48–49, 51–54, 86–87; GED resources development by, 43; generation one test findings of, 69–71; generation one test findings revisions of, 71–72; generation two testing of, 79, *80*; IRB challenges of, 38–39; jail branch observation and participation of, 92–94; LARA first encounter of, 8–9; LARA first meeting of, 24–25; LARA's teaching context researched by, 44–45, 87; lessons learned by, 103–4; new teaching context writing of, 86–88; observation perception of, 90; on Purdue and class identity, 7; researcher idea of, 89–90; service learning challenges and limitations need of, 121–24, 132; service motivation of, 6; stage one and two budget of, 40; Sunrise Diner meeting with Sam, 73–76; UAB diverse stakeholder communication of, 120–21; as UAB writing center director, 115–19, 132; on working at Maize, 7–8; WPA of, 116–17, 125n6; Writing in Birmingham service-learning project of, 122–23
Wells Fargo Bank, 124n1
West Lafayette, Indiana, 2
WiderNet Project, University of Iowa, 18
WinWay Resume Deluxe, 33, 76, 78
Words on the Go, 18
Workforce Investment Act, 31
Workforce Investment Board, 27
WorkOne Express, 15, 20–21, 41, 47, 66, 85–86; assessment of participant writing for, 81–83, 83n3; building and area surrounding, 17; client descriptions of, 74; coordinator and volunteers duties at, 33; CWEST usability findings on, 80–81; CWEST use by, 101–2; description of, 31–32; determining needs and willingness of, 16, 18; developing resources for, 78–79; employment assistance software and other resources of, 33; employment percentages of, 34; end-user participants in, 97–98; face-to-face services at, 32–33; goals of, 32; independent raters of résumés used in, 82, 83n4, 102; iterative design process of, 75–76; lack of staffing in, 76; LARA partnership with, 31; longstanding role of, 16–17; operating budget for, 33; OWL revised posting on, 79; project proposal to, 35; recession affects on, 127; research on, 23–24; resource development for, 78–79; Roosevelt's New Deal regarding, 31; serious mood of, 32; technology use of staff and clients at, 76–78; total user numbers in, 33; unemployment figures of, 74
Workplace Investment Act, 27
WPA. *See* writing program administration
"The WPA as Father, Husband, Ex" (Hesse), 117–18
writing centers, 1, 3–4, 12, 87, 125n6; civic engagement role of, 124, 129, 131–32; community-based research in, 104, 124, 131; community engagement connection with, 120, 130–31; expressing failure in, 120; missions of, 2; university-community collaboration in, 41, 101, 133
Writing Lab, Purdue, 16–18, 117; capstone project proposal submitted

to, 34–35; ILR similarity in, 30; LARA differences and similarities with, 30, 45, 87

writing program administration (WPA), 116–17, 125n6

York Road Literacy and Employment Initiative (YRLEI): addressing of skills in literacy and technology in, 112–13; Brizee coding and analyzing data of, 112; Caranante as research assistant in, 110–13; community adoption of, 114–15; CWEST project guidance of, 108–9; four phases of, 109; GEDCO/CARES data tracking of, 112; GEDCO/CARES usability testing and workshops with, 110; Kolvenbach award of, 110; literacy and employment issues focus of, 107–8; longitudinal data use in, 115; participant recruitment and retention in, 113–14; participant reimbursement in, 114, 125n5; partners of, 109; project budget of, 110–11; qualitative and quantitative data collection in, 110–11; RSNA collaboration with, 110; timeline of, 109–10

Young Women's Christian Association (YWCA), 26

YRLEI. *See* York Road Literacy and Employment Initiative

YWCA of Greater Lafayette, 26

YWCA Reading Academy, 26, 27

About the Authors

Allen Brizee is associate professor of writing in the writing department at Loyola University Maryland. At Loyola, he teaches courses in first-year composition, rhetoric, professional writing, and writing for the Web, and he also coordinates the writing internship program. Allen integrates service-learning into many of his writing courses; he and his students have collaborated with local community members and nonprofit organizations in Baltimore City since spring 2011. For this work, Allen received the 2015 Loyola Faculty Award for Excellence in Engaged Scholarship. He has published in the *Journal of Technical Writing and Communication*; *Across the Disciplines: A Journal of Language, Learning, and Academic Writing*; *Computers and Composition: An International Journal*; and he has published in edited collections.

Jaclyn M. Wells is assistant professor of English at the University of Alabama at Birmingham (UAB). She directs the university writing center and teaches tutoring pedagogy courses, first-year composition, and professional writing. A participant in UAB's faculty fellows in engaged scholarship program, Jaclyn regularly teaches service-learning and has partnered with area schools, libraries, and nonprofits. Jaclyn's work has appeared in the *Community Literacy Journal*; *Reflections*; *WPA: Writing Program Administration*; and various edited collections.

www.ingramcontent.com/pod-product-compliance
Lightning Source LLC
Chambersburg PA
CBHW030113010526
44116CB00005B/227